T0331792

Agent–Based Modeling in Humanitarian Interventions:

Emerging Research and Opportunities

John McCaskill
University of Texas at Dallas, USA

A volume in the Advances in Electronic Government, Digital Divide, and Regional Development (AEGDDRD) Book Series

www.igi-global.com

Published in the United States of America by
  IGI Global
  Information Science Reference (an imprint of IGI Global)
  701 E. Chocolate Avenue
  Hershey PA 17033
  Tel: 717-533-8845
  Fax: 717-533-8661
  E-mail: cust@igi-global.com
  Web site: http://www.igi-global.com

Library of Congress Cataloging-in-Publication Data

Names: McCaskill, John, 1960- author.
Title: Agent-based modeling in humanitarian interventions : emerging research
  and opportunities / by John McCaskill.
Description: Hershey, PA : Information Science Reference, [2017]
Identifiers: LCCN 2016044527| ISBN 9781522517825 (hardcover) | ISBN
  9781522517832 (ebook)
Subjects: LCSH: International agencies--Security measures. | Nongovernmental
  organizations--Security measures. | Humanitarian assistance. | Human
  security. | Risk management. | Insurgency. | Counterinsurgency.
Classification: LCC JZ4841 .M4155 2017 | DDC 362.88--dc23 LC record available at https://lccn.
loc.gov/2016044527

This book is published in the IGI Global book series Advances in Electronic Government, Digital Divide, and Regional Development (AEGDDRD) (ISSN: 2326-9103; eISSN: 2326-9111)

British Cataloguing in Publication Data
A Cataloguing in Publication record for this book is available from the British Library.

Advances in Electronic Government, Digital Divide, and Regional Development (AEGDDRD) Book Series

ISSN:2326-9103
EISSN:2326-9111

Edtior-in-Chief: Zaigham Mahmood, University of Derby, UK & North West University, South Africa

MISSION

The successful use of digital technologies (including social media and mobile technologies) to provide public services and foster economic development has become an objective for governments around the world. The development towards electronic government (or e-government) not only affects the efficiency and effectiveness of public services, but also has the potential to transform the nature of government interactions with its citizens. Current research and practice on the adoption of electronic/digital government and the implementation in organizations around the world aims to emphasize the extensiveness of this growing field.

The **Advances in Electronic Government, Digital Divide & Regional Development (AEGDDRD)** book series aims to publish authored, edited and case books encompassing the current and innovative research and practice discussing all aspects of electronic government development, implementation and adoption as well the effective use of the emerging technologies (including social media and mobile technologies) for a more effective electronic governance (or e-governance).

COVERAGE

- Issues and Challenges in E-Government Adoption
- Adoption of Innovation with Respect to E-Government
- Case Studies and Practical Approaches to E-Government and E-Governance
- E-Government in Developing Countries and Technology Adoption
- Public Information Management, Regional Planning, Rural Development
- Citizens Participation and Adoption of E-Government Provision
- Social Media, Web 2.0, and Mobile Technologies in E-Government
- Frameworks and Methodologies for E-Government Development
- Current Research and Emerging Trends in E-Government Development
- E-Governance and Use of Technology for Effective Government

IGI Global is currently accepting manuscripts for publication within this series. To submit a proposal for a volume in this series, please contact our Acquisition Editors at Acquisitions@igi-global.com or visit: http://www.igi-global.com/publish/.

Titles in this Series

For a list of additional titles in this series, please visit:
http://www.igi-global.com/book-series/advances-educational-technologies-instructional-design/73678

Population Growth and Rapid Urbanization in the Developing World
Umar G. Benna (Ahmadu Bello Univ., Nigeria) and Shaibu Bala Garba (Qatar Univ., Qatar)
Information Science Reference • ©2016 • 358pp • H/C (ISBN: 9781522501879) • US $205.00

Political Discourse in Emergent, Fragile, and Failed Democracies
Daniel Ochieng Orwenjo (Technical Univ. of Kenya, Kenya) Omondi Oketch (Technical Univ. of Kenya, Kenya) and Asiru Hameed Tunde (Umaru Musa Yar'adua Univ., Nigeria)
Information Science Reference • ©2016 • 412pp • H/C (ISBN: 9781522500810) • US $185.00

International Perspectives on Socio-Economic Development in the Era of Globalization
Saurabh Sen (Sunbeam College for Women, India) Anshuman Bhattacharya (Sunbeam College for Women, India) and Ruchi Sen (Sunbeam College for Women, India)
Business Science Reference • ©2016 • 288pp • H/C (ISBN: 9781466699083) • US $175.00

Comparative Political and Economic Perspectives on the MENA Region
M. Mustafa Erdoğdu (Marmara Univ., Turkey) and Bryan Christiansen (PryMarke, LLC, USA)
Information Science Reference • ©2016 • 386pp • H/C (ISBN: 9781466696013) • US $205.00

Handbook of Research on Entrepreneurial Success and its Impact on Regional Development
Luísa Carvalho (Universidade Aberta, Portugal & CEFAGE, Universidade de Évora, Portugal)
Information Science Reference • ©2016 • 878pp • H/C (ISBN: 9781466695672) • US $430.00

Trends, Prospects, and Challenges in Asian E-Governance
Inderjeet Singh Sodhi (St. Wilfred's P.G. College, India)
Information Science Reference • ©2016 • 410pp • H/C (ISBN: 9781466695368) • US $190.00

Handbook of Research on Comparative Approaches to the Digital Age Revolution....
Brasilina Passarelli (School of Communications and Arts, University of São Paulo, Brazil) Joseph Straubhaar (The University of Texas at Austin, USA) and Aurora Cuevas-Cerveró (Complutense University of Madrid, Spain)
Information Science Reference • ©2016 • 530pp • H/C (ISBN: 9781466687400) • US $325.00

www.igi-global.com

701 East Chocolate Avenue, Hershey, PA 17033, USA
Tel: 717-533-8845 x100 • Fax: 717-533-8661
E-Mail: cust@igi-global.com • www.igi-global.com

Table of Contents

Preface

Troubled nations pose a complex dilemma for policy makers in international organizations. The humanitarian urge to intervene to relieve suffering is strong but it also has a dark side. The delivery of aid to a distressed population in a troubled nation is never neutral: there are always winners and losers. The difficulty in formulating policy lies in the complexity of these types of scenarios. The cause and effect are frequently widely separated in either time or space. Compounding the complexity are the multiple feedback loops surrounding the problem. It is frequently impossible to determine which feedback loop provided the correct linkage between cause and effect until the scenario has played itself out.

The purpose of this study is to identify behavior patterns for the various entities operating among the population where there are varying degrees of stability operations being conducted and utilize these patterns in creation of behavioral models. Agent-based modeling is derived from complexity science. If complexity cannot be readily defined, some of the behavioral elements can be defined. The behavioral elements derived from the literature review are utilized to create the behavioral rules that the agents, or adaptive actors utilize in the simulations. Agent based modeling utilizes five principles that guide development:

1. Simple rules guide agent behavior and can generate complex behaviors;
2. There is no single agent that directs the other agents – there is no agent hierarchy;
3. Each agent has bounded rationality in that each can only respond to local situations in the environment and other agents in close proximity;
4. There is no global rule for agent behavior; and,
5. Emergent behavior is demonstrated by any behaviors that occur above the level of the individual (Kiel, 2005; Langton, 1989).

From these principles, agent-based modeling builds a macro social interactive structure from the interaction of individual units from the bottom-up versus the top-down approach typically taken in typical social science studies (Epstein & Axtell, 1996).

These types of simulations could provide a viable method for assessing risk of various strategic and operational strategies as well as reducing the level of uncertainty associated with counterinsurgency and stability operations. The promise of allowing analysis of patterns of structural emergence and destruction is real and provides an improved adaptive response to the environment (Kiel, 2005). These agent behavioral models are utilized in agent based modeling simulations to help identify emergent behavioral outcomes of the agents in the population. By varying the level of coordination between the NGOs and the Governmental agents (United Nations Development Program, USAID, military), different strategies can be identified to increase the effectiveness of those agents and the utilization of resources in the execution of rebuilding a war torn society. This dissertation uses agent based modeling to run simulations involving NGO / government coordination policies and their effects during stability / counterinsurgency operations. The goal is to develop a better understanding of whether a high level of coordination between military and NGO activities have a force multiplying effect. Further conditions examined are: Does the level of violence present in the area of operations or the levels of legitimacy for both the indigenous government and/or the insurgency movement, have an impact on the levels of effectiveness – if any – derived from this military-NGO coordination?

Within this study, a generalized and abstract theory of the interaction of the military and civilian NGOs is derived from the views of the participants through the literature on this interaction process. The goal is to maximize the similarities and differences of the information within the emerging categories, and from those differences, revise and present parameter estimates for dealing with the vague, uncertain, confusing, and ambiguous interface between the military and the civilian NGO stratum (Creswell, 2009). The simulation is conducted in conditions described in Roberts (2010) quadrant IV diagram: low domain consensus between agents and a high level of martial threat to all the agents involved. The simulation resource in the landscape for this study is the support of the indigenous population. The following are the agent types and their rules for the simulation. There are be two levels of violence set - low and high – for each set of agent rule parameters.

- International governmental agents whose rules vary with different policy initiatives: high levels of coordination, no coordination, and subjugation of either the civilian or military agencies by the other.
- International governmental, local government and insurgent agent numbers vary (low, medium, and high) for each policy initiative.
- Local governmental agents have three rules regarding the legitimacy interaction with the population: low, medium, and high levels of legitimacy defined by the governmental agents' likelihood to reproduce (recruit additional members from the population).
- Insurgent agents have three rules regarding the legitimacy interaction with the population: low, medium, and high levels of legitimacy defined by the insurgent agents' likelihood to reproduce (recruit additional members from the population).

The landscape (local population) initial conditions of being are in one of three states: loyal to the local government, neutral, or loyal to the insurgency. The three states of the population are randomly distributed in roughly equal proportion.

This study focuses on two concepts: the characteristics of the policies available to United Nations agencies in conducting stability and / or counterinsurgency operations and the delivery of development aid and the characteristics of the NGOs engaged in the delivery of development aid in the same operating areas. The categories of case studies of policy that have been examined for this study are:

- Police in the lead with military support or vice versa (Sepp, 2004).
- The timing of development aid delivery vis-à-vis the stage of the counterinsurgency campaign – either early or late (Barlow, 2010).
- The integration of local population into security forces – either high or low (Barton, 2010; Megahan, 2010; Sepp, 2004).
- The level of local population inclusion in development aid delivery – either high or low (Brinkerhoff, 2010; Guttieri, 2010; Pimbo, 2010).
- The level of local institutional development - either high or low (Brinkerhoff, 2010; Pandya, 2010; Sepp, 2004; von Hippel, 2010).
- The level of security from violence – either high or low (Guttieri, 2010; Sepp, 2004).
- The level of local population cooperation with counterinsurgency forces vis-à-vis the insurgents - either high or low (Galula, 1964).

The categories for the characteristics of NGOs that have been identified at this point are:

- The level of coordination with government agencies – either high or low (Curry, 2010; Szanyna et al., 2009).
- The propensity to operate independently from other organizations either NGO or governmental – either high or low (de Haan, 2009; Flanigan, 2010).
- The religious affiliation of the NGO – either affiliated.

These characteristics are utilized in building agent based modeling simulations. Their relative impact in describing the initial conditions of the simulation (to establish the mathematical relationships for programming) is determined and inserted in the agent based model equations to control the magnitude of the relationship between variables.

The agent based modeling simulations utilize parameter estimates derived in the method described above as a general starting point. The current Afghan counterinsurgency scenario is used to set the initial conditions for the simulation. With this baseline established, additional simulations are run that vary the policy parameters in accordance with the options available to policy makers as described in the previous paragraphs. The outcomes of the simulations are captured with particular emphasis placed upon the interface dynamics between the groups and the effects of those dynamics on the outcomes observed.

The modeling software to be used for the simulations is NetLogo. NetLogo was developed by Uri Wilensky in 1999 at the Center for Connected Learning and Computer-Based Modeling. It is the agent based modeling software that is used to run the simulations. This software is designed to simulate social phenomena in a programmable modeling environment. The software should be well suited to this research because it allows instructions to be given to hundreds or even thousands of agents which can all operate independently making it possible to explore the linkages between macro-level patterns of emergent behavior and the micro-level behavior of individuals. NetLogo also allows for simulations to be opened and the conditions varied which are critical to exploring agent behavior and scenario outcomes when policy changes are made and introduced. The software also allows for a multitude of graphic representations of the outputs which are extremely useful in presenting the findings of this research (Wilensky, 1999). There have been some fascinating studies on how foreign aid, NGOs, and diplomacy work together (or at odds) in foreign development and national security (Lacquement, 2010).

Flanigan (2010) has conducted a study of how NGOs can frequently be very partisan in strife ridden areas causing them to be problematic for cooperative associations with United Nations agencies. Roberts (2010) has conducted a review of where the current state of affairs has progressed. While providing a framework to understand the depth and breadth of the issues involved, the thrust of her work calls for additional research into the appropriate methodologies for dealing with "The Civilian-Military Conundrum in the Post-Cold War Era" (Roberts, 2010, p. 213).

While in some cases, these studies have provided a great depth of information on how NGOs function along with their interaction with the populations they are providing assistance. In other cases there have been very broad surveys of why population centric counterinsurgency operations are a critical capability that should be resident within the Department of Defense (DOD). Sara Lischer has been examining the challenges being faced when integration of NGOs into the planning process in nation building does not take place. Nancy Roberts, a professor of defense analysis at the Naval Post-graduate School in Monterey, has recently published an article lamenting this very issue (Roberts, 2010). Roberts suggest that one of the main issues is the "bleeding boundary" between the military and civilian NGO roles in providing services to distressed populations. From her article, the crux of the issue is the new field manual on COIN that has the military displacing the NGOs in the domain of providing humanitarian relief and thereby causing domain consensus to disappear and friction between the groups to escalate.

The problem unfortunately is not as simple as establishing domain consensus. The varieties of NGOs that can be operating in any given area form their own mosaic of goals and intentions. Some of these goals align with those of the interests of the United States – and therefore with the U. S. military – while others may be diametrically opposed. The problem then, for the military commander and other governmental organizations, becomes multifaceted yet the objective remains singular; the population. Even the basic and critical activity of identifying friend from foe, for all organizations involved, becomes complex and constantly shifting. There is a lack of synergy across disciplines in the study of how to establish where the common goals lie and how they can be effectively integrated (Franke & Guttieri, 2009). Additionally, this integration needs to occur without adversely affecting the ability of each of the organizations involved to operate effectively in accomplishing its goals (Mann, 2008; United States Institute of Peace and Peacekeeping, 2009; United States Africa Command 2009 Posture Statement).

ORGANIZATION OF THE BOOK

The study described in this book utilizes the recent international coalition efforts to stabilize Afghanistan as the backdrop for the simulation experiment. While there are some very Afghan specific data used to build the landscape for this research simulation, they serve to inform more broadly applicable latent variables that can be found in many "troubled state" scenarios. Several components of background and theory are covered to address the research question with the literature review being the first element. The introductory literature review in Chapter 1 contains a brief examination of the ethical choices facing policy makers in stability and nation building operations. From there a review of the change capacity of Afghan society and how it limits the policy goals of international intervention is conducted (the current policy environment chosen to provide the baseline for the model's landscape). Chapter 2 contains a more in depth literature review that includes the roles that the military, NGOs, and complexity theory play in the study.

Chapter 3 reviews the methodology used in the study including a discussion of origin of the parameters and rule sets used to conduct the simulation. Chapter 4 fully presents the model itself in the ODD protocol (Overview, Design concepts, and Details), which contains the data analysis of the model runs and the outcomes of the statistical tests on the parameter sets. The final chapter contains policy implications, conclusions, and suggestions for further research.

REFERENCES

Barlow, D. (2010). *The Kuwait task force: Post conflict planning and interagency coordination.* Washington, DC: NDU Center for Complex Operations. Retrieved February 4, 2011, from http://www.nps.edu/Academics/AcademicGroups/GPPAG/Documents/PDF/Education%20and%20Research/Research%20Outputs/Case_4_Kuwait_Task_Force.pdf

Barton, F. D. (2010). Setting rule of law priorities in the early days of an intervention. In F. D. Kramer, T. Dempsey, J. Gregoire & S. Merrill (Eds.), *Civil power in irregular conflict* (pp. 149-158). Washington, DC: Center for Naval Analyses, US Army Peacekeeping and Stability Operations Institute and Association of the US Army. Retrieved February 4, 2011, from http://www.cna.org/research/2010/civil-power-irregular-conflict

Creswell, J. W. (2009). *Research design: Qualitative, quantitative, and mixed methods approaches*. Thousand Oaks, CA: Sage Publications, Inc.

Curry, P. (2010). *Dynamic tension: Security, stability and the opium trade*. Washington, DC: NDU Center for Complex Operations. Retrieved February 4, 2011, from http://www.nps.edu/Academics/AcademicGroups/GPPAG/Documents/PDF/Education%20and%20Research/Research%20Outputs/2_Dynamic_Tension.pdf

de Haan, A. (2009). *How the aid industry works: An introduction to international development*. Sterling, VA: Kumarian Press.

Epstein, J. M., & Axtell, R. (1996). *Growing artificial societies: Social science from the bottom up*. Washington, DC: Brookings Institution Press.

Flanigan, S. (2010). *For the love of god: NGOS and religious identity in a violent world*. Sterling, VA: Kumarian Press.

Franke, V. C., & Guttieri, K. (2009). Picking up the pieces: Are United States officers ready for nation building? *Journal of Political and Military Sociology, 37*(1), 1–25.

Galula, D. (1964). *Counterinsurgency warfare: Theory and Practice*. Westport, CT: Praeger Security International.

Guttieri, K. (2010). Interim governments in theory and practice after protracted conflict. In F. D. Kramer, T. Dempsey, J. Gregoire & S. Merrill (Eds.), *Civil power in irregular conflict* (pp. 51 - 56). Washington, DC: Center for Naval Analyses, US Army Peacekeeping and Stability Operations Institute and Association of the US Army. Retrieved February 4, 2011, from http://www.cna.org/research/2010/civil-power-irregular-conflict

Kiel, L. D. (2005). A primer for agent-based modeling in public administration: Exploring complexity in "would-be" administrative worlds. *Public Administration Quarterly, 29*(3), 268–296.

Lacquement, R. A. (2010). Integrating civilian and military activities. *Parameters, 1*(Spring), 20–33.

Langton, C. (1989). Artificial life. In Artificial Life, the Proceedings of an Interdisciplinary Workshop on the Synthesis and Simulation of Living Systems. Redwood City, CA: Addison Wesley.

Lischer, S. K. (2005). *Dangerous sanctuaries: Refugee camps, civil war, and the dilemmas of humanitarian aid*. Ithaca, NY: Cornell University Press.

Lischer, S. K. (2007). Military intervention and the "force multiplier". *Global Governance, 13*, 99–118.

Megahan, R. (2010). Achieving immediate developmental change in host-nation police. In F. D. Kramer, T. Dempsey, J. Gregoire & S. Merrill (Eds.), *Civil power in irregular conflict* (pp. 97 - 112). Washington, DC: Center for Naval Analyses, US Army Peacekeeping and Stability Operations Institute and Association of the US Army. Retrieved February 4, 2011, from http://www.cna.org/research/2010/civil-power-irregular-conflict

Pimbo, J. (2010). *Military provision of humanitarian and civic assistance: A day in the life of a civil affairs team in the Horn of Africa.* Washington, DC: NDU Center for Complex Operations. Retrieved February 4, 2011, from http://www.nps.edu/Academics/AcademicGroups/GPPAG/Documents/PDF/Education%20and%20Research/Research%20Outputs/Case_5_Humanitarian_Assistance.pdf

Roberts, N. C. (2010). Spanning bleeding boundaries: Humanitarianism, NGOs, and the civilian-military nexus in the post-cold war era. *Public Administration Review, 70*(March), 212–222. doi:10.1111/j.1540-6210.2010.02135_2.x

Sepp, K. I. (2005, October). Best practices in counterinsurgency. Military Review, 8-12.

Szayna, T. S., Eaton, D., Barnett, J. E., II, Lawson, B. S., Kelly, T. K., & Haldeman, Z. (2009). *Integrating civilian agencies in stability operations.* Santa Monica, CA: Rand. Retrieved June 19, 2010, from http://www.rand.org/pubs/monographs/2009/RAND_MG801.pdf

United States Institute of Peace and Peacekeeping. (2009). *Guiding principles for stabilization and reconstruction.* Washington, DC: Author.

Wilensky, U. (1999). *NetLogo.* Center for Connected Learning and Computer-Based Modeling, Northwestern University. Retrieved February 4, 2011, from http://ccl.northwestern.edu/netlogo/

Acknowledgment

The author would like to acknowledge the help of all the people involved in this project and, more specifically, to the colleagues at The University of Texas at Dallas and the anonymous reviewers that took part in the review process. Without their support, this book would not have become a reality.

John McCaskill
The University of Texas at Dallas, USA

Chapter 1
Introduction

INTRODUCTION

Conflict within a nation state is frequently accompanied by a humanitarian crisis. Internally displaced persons, hunger, disease, and other maladies conspire to tear the fabric of a society apart. While the first instinct of many in the international community is to help, that help can lead to trouble. Human interaction is highly complex yet our capacity to make sense of it all is limited. This state of affairs frequently causes the world community to stand by and let the upheaval take its course, and only then attempt to pick up the pieces of a broken society if things work out poorly. Even in the best case, the provision of aid has the potential to prolong the conflict. We cannot readily forecast the outcomes of intervention because our top-down models have difficulties dealing with the complex interactions associated with these types of events. Bottom-up approaches are not necessarily any better at prediction, but they do have the capacity to provide insights into the interaction of the variables involved in complex humanitarian interventions; much like a flight simulator allows a pilot to try various procedural options when presented with a system failure.

BACKGROUND

The international community has become more attuned to the number of complex humanitarian issues developing throughout the world (United Na-

DOI: 10.4018/978-1-5225-1782-5.ch001

tions General Assembly Resolution 52/167, 1998). This is particularly true in parts of the developing world where civil war or some other driver of civil strife overwhelms the region's capacity for emergency response. When this occurs, the international community feels obligated to act as stated in a series of Guiding Principles contained within the United Nations General Assembly resolution 46/182 (1992):

The magnitude and duration of many emergencies may be beyond the response capacity of many affected countries. International cooperation to address emergency situations and to strengthen the response capacity of affected countries is thus of great importance. ... Intergovernmental and non-governmental organizations working impartially and with strictly humanitarian motives should continue to make a significant contribution in supplementing national efforts. ... There is a clear relationship between emergency, rehabilitation and development. In order to ensure a smooth transition from relief to rehabilitation and development, emergency assistance should be provided in ways that will be supportive of recovery and long-term development. (Annex, p. 50)

MAIN FOCUS OF THE CHAPTER

For this study, the statement above is the operationalized definition of stability: the effort to address complex humanitarian emergencies in a way that supplements and rebuilds the receiving nation's capacity to take care of its citizens. This international effort can include, but is not limited to providing security and development aid, assisting with the establishment or reestablishment of the rule of law and governance, as well as humanitarian assistance.

Policy makers face a conundrum in failed or failing nation states: how to provide humanitarian relief while weaving the torn fabric of a society back together. Humanitarian action alone is rarely neutral. The advance of humanitarian care and supplies frequently frees belligerents to militarize the refugees and continue the conflict on a wider scale. Other times it takes on a "placebo effect" and nullifies the impetus to provide the military or political engagement necessary to address the cause of the strife (Lischer, 2007). Policy makers that lead with military forces acting as humanitarian workers (such as the Provisional Reconstruction Teams operating in Afghanistan) often find they cannot create the stability they hope for due to inadequate security. Lischer describes the military planners' goal as gaining a "force multiplier effect" from engaging in humanitarian operations. This force multiplier effect is quite simply an increase in efficiency; an ability to do more with fewer resources. They are perhaps limited in their view by current counterinsurgency theory which suggests that by winning the "hearts and minds" of the population, the security concerns will begin to take care of themselves (FM 3-24, 2007; Galula, 1964). The basis of the theory is that if the population can be turned against the insurgents, then the insurgents' base of power is eliminated and the foot soldiers of the movement will be either melded back into the population or be apprehended. Either way, the insurgency is defeated. The difficulty arises when the question of legitimacy comes to bare. Are the insurgents a group of extremists or do they represent unaddressed grievances with the current governing factions? A deeper question then becomes, "How can international agencies help to establish a system of governance in a war torn society without exacerbating the issues that caused the strife to begin with?"

If policy makers wish to effectively influence the decisions of others, is coercion through the threat of direct military force the only method available? Alternatively, is there hope of using "libertarian paternalism" to effectively frame choices that cause worrisome groups to make the right decisions (Thaler & Sunstein, 2008)? The fundamental principle is that development plans formulated in one culture can have unexpected outcomes when implemented in another because the beneficiaries view reality from a very different cultural paradigm (Portes, 2010). Multiple parties become involved with varying degrees of conflicting interests and objectives: military forces are looking to win hearts and minds in an effort to enhance security (Galula, 1964); nongovernmental organizations (NGOs) strive to maintain their core values of neutrality, impartiality, and independence (Lischer, 2007); the degree of "Domain Conflict" between the military forces and the civilian aid NGOs providing humanitarian assistance within the same operating area (Roberts, 2010). This latter issue is represented in Figure 1. Humanitarian Relief as shown in Figure 1 is the mode of international intervention where military forces provide logistics assets to NGOs and the NGOs in turn, utilize their institutional capacity to deliver the aid to those determined to have the greatest need (Roberts, 2010). Peacekeeping becomes more conflicted because the level of violence (or the threat of violence) is increased.

Peacekeeping is defined as the "monitoring and enforcing a cease-fire agreed to by two or more former combatants. It proceeds in an atmosphere where peace exists and where the former combatants minimally prefer peace to continued war" (Snow, 1993, p. 7). As the level of violence increases further, international forces are inserted into a situation where a cease fire does not exist and may not be desired by one or both sides of the conflict. This increases the level of domain conflict between NGOs and international

Figure 1. Humanitarian relief

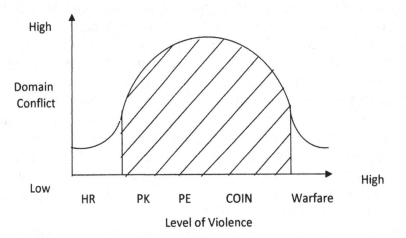

forces because the appearance of neutrality begins to fray: "they [international forces] are active fighters who must impose a cease-fire that is opposed by one or both combatants; in the process, the neutrality that distinguishes peacekeepers will most likely be lost" (Snow, 1993, p. 7). Counterinsurgency has no pretense of neutrality and has the international community taking sides. This is the down side of the slope policy makers can find themselves on when participating in complex humanitarian interventions.

Then the question of change capacity within the targeted society must be addressed: "How much change is tolerable and how fast can it be introduced into the fractured society before the change effort itself becomes the cause of the instability and strife within the culture?" If pushed too far, too quickly, the legitimacy of the internationally backed indigenous government rapidly decreases as resistance to change increases. The stakes for these types of interventions are extremely high for all parties involved. Proponents of intervention frequently sight the moral responsibility of the community of nations. Unfortunately the moral clarity these voices have in the concept of intervention to save innocent life frequently run into the ethical vagaries of reality (Valentino, 2011). The difficulties lie in answering the question of how to intervene in these types of arenas. In most cases, as Lischer emphasizes, it is almost impossible to make a completely neutral intervention. When attempting to help victims of human rights abuses, the intervention frequently empowers armed factions representing (or claiming to represent) these same victims. Unfortunately, these factions are often implicated in human rights abuses of their own (Valentino, 2011). This unfortunate reality causes one of the first casualties of intervention: moral clarity.

The NATO bombing campaign in Kosovo provides an example of the problems encountered. In 1999, NATO air power helped push Serbian forces from Kosovo. Unfortunately, the former victims turned on the remaining Serbian civilians and killed hundreds while forcing thousands to run for their lives (Valentino, 2011, p. 63). There have been repeated calls for the investigation of the leaders of the Kosovo Liberation Army for crimes against humanity. Another type of problem was exemplified when United Nations forces intervened in Somalia in 1993. It is widely remembered in the West that eighteen American soldiers were killed during the "Black Hawk Down" incident but the other uncomfortable fact is that at least 500 Somalis were killed with over half of them being women and children (Valentino, 2011, p. 64). What seem like simple solutions to humanitarian crises often have complex and counter intuitive outcomes. When one side is suddenly empowered by outside intervention, it frequently turns its pent up wrath on the other. In other instances, the outside intervention becomes an additional cause of death and destruction of innocents instead of being their saviors.

Another issue to be considered in interventions is the monetary costs. For the United States alone, the cost for the military mission was more than seven billion dollars and resulted in saving between 10,000 and 25,000 lives (Valentino, 2011, p. 67). Those expenditures equated to spending between 280,000 and 700,000 dollars for each life saved. Currently in Afghanistan, the United States has budgeted 555 billion dollars for operations in 2012 alone. The United States is spending almost 18,500 dollars for every man, woman, and child living in Afghanistan which has a total population of just under thirty million (CIA World Factbook, 2012). Stremlau (1998) contends, in a report commissioned by the Carnegie Corporation, that early and robust efforts at intervention would be more cost effective. The problem is identifying complex humanitarian emergencies that will respond positively to action by the world community and then only intervene in those cases. Again, the track record on this type of undertaking is poor. Valentino provides a graphic example.

One of the most tragic aspects of the genocides in Bosnia, Rwanda, and Darfur was that international peacekeepers were present during some of the worst episodes of violence, such as the slaughter of some 8,000 Bosnian Muslims in Srebrenica in 1995, which was witnessed by 400 UN peacekeepers. The problem in these cases was not that no one was sent to prevent the violence; it was that the forces that were deployed were not given the resources or mandates to stop the violence breaking out around them. (Valentino, 2011, p. 68)

Many analysts including Lischer, Roberts, and Stremlau have suggested that better coordination between military forces and the NGO community would bring about better outcomes in these types of interventions. Such coordination would reduce the domain conflicts Roberts warns of as well as reducing the placebo effect the Lischer describes. By each organization somehow coordinating with each other, each would become more efficient and effective, providing that force multiplier effect implementation planners are always searching for. This is the policy area this study investigates.

The question then becomes one of integration. The understanding and integration of military force with NGOs in the area of operations are critical to reestablishing stability within a fractured society. Will the United Nations' agencies be met with a handshake or a fist by the populations they are attempting to help? Understanding the military-NGO interaction is a crucial item of policy framework that will determine feasible courses of action to international governmental agencies. Further, what level and type of integration should be attempted? At present, United Nations agencies have no clear structure or formal process for determining how to either integrate the efforts of NGOs with coincident military interests or neutralize NGOs with counter interests. This lack of structure is thought to reduce the effectiveness of stability and development efforts both in terms of direct and indirect mission success. Additionally, these issues exhibit non-linear behavior. Unexpected events – such as the Sunni awakening in Iraq - may change the course of history. It seems that small differences in inputs can become enormous differences in output. This phenomenon is referred to by James Gleick (1988, p. 8) as a "sensitive dependence on initial conditions." These are the type of problems that defy explanation by traditional top-down theories of social reality. This dissertation tests the theory that a high level of coordination between military and NGO operations can be a force multiplier in the effort to bring stability to a strife torn region. The research question is: "Does a high level of coordination between military and NGO activities have a force multiplying effect?" Further conditions examined are: "Does the level of violence present in the area of operations or the levels of legitimacy for both the indigenous government and the insurgency movement, have an impact on the levels of effectiveness – if any – derived from this military-NGO coordination."

ISSUES DESCRIBED IN THE LITERATURE

Military

International efforts to enforce peace and reassemble the fabric of a conflict torn society are complex by their very nature. There are multiple parties involved with varying degrees of conflicting interests and objectives. Military forces are looking to win hearts and minds (Galula, 1964) while NGOs are steadfast in their desire to hold on to their core values of neutrality, impartiality, and independence. All of these issues are further complicated when overlaid upon the question of change capacity within the targeted society. Given these interdependencies and conflicting objectives, distilling out a clear picture of the interaction of all the variables presents a challenge.

Motivations across actors are heterogeneous. The actors in strife ridden areas have motivations that form a mosaic from the bottom up, not top down. Again, the complexity of the interactions of various actors in these areas can lead to unforeseen outcomes and the outcomes are extremely sensitive to variations in initial conditions. The Comprehensive Strategy for Malakand, also known as the Malakand Pilot Project, is an important example of how external actors can support locally owned and operated reconstruction and stabilization (United States Institute of Peace and Peacekeeping, 2009). The Guiding Principles for Stabilization and Reconstruction is the first strategic doctrine ever produced for civilian planners and practitioners involved in peace-building missions. This document provides useful background information from the U.S. Department of State's perspective (Civilian Response 2010). The point of view that these initiatives must be locally owned and operated to be successful is a critical shift in paradigm for a governmental agency. Many governmental agencies, especially the U.S. Department of Defense, are still in the mode of winning hearts and minds through the use of military led actions units such as the Provincial Reconstruction Teams that are currently in use in Afghanistan (Roberts, 2010; FM 3-24, 2006).

The use of PRTs is an offshoot of the writings of David Galula (1964). Galula was a French Infantry officer involved in counterinsurgency operations in China, French Indo China, and Algeria (Nagl, 2006). At the time of his writing, he was posted as a Visiting Fellow at Harvard University. His work on counterinsurgency warfare is one of the prime references cited in the Army / Marine Corps field manual on counterinsurgency operations, FM 3-24. Galula writes from a mechanistic and ethically neutral perspective in that he describes in very calculating terms how to turn a population against an insurgent, thereby destroying the insurgents' source of power. He identifies the center of gravity (the origin of the belligerents' source of power) for both the insurgent and the counterinsurgent as the population itself. From his perspective, protecting the population from harm is not an act of humanity; it is an act of expediency. The battle is joined literally to win over the goodwill of the population. The amount and quality of intelligence, or information, about the insurgents' activities that is forthcoming from the population, is the scorecard of measure. His capstone argument is that if the population feels more secure by cooperating with the counterinsurgent forces, then the insurgent has lost and can be relatively quickly eradicated from the scene. On the other hand, if the population lives in fear of the insurgents' reprisal for cooperating with the counterinsurgent forces (or the established local government agencies), then the counterinsurgent forces are condemned to chasing shadows in a self-defeating effort to counter idealism with lethal force.

Gian Gentile (2009) takes a completely different view as he rails against the adaptation of FM 3-24 by the U. S. Army. He is adamant in his opposition to the military involvement in nation building. The main points of his thesis are that the military does not have the resident expertise to perform nation building effectively and that the effort to gain such expertise will be paid for by a loss of combat readiness. This position sets him in direct opposition to Galula and Nagl (2005) which helps to frame the issue of military involvement in the provision of social services in reconstruction operations. His seemingly lone voice of opposition from the position of the West Point Historian is uniquely powerful and useful.

Goode (2009) provides a fascinating look at the force requirements to execute a counterinsurgency strategy. He derives a formula that basically shows that if enough manpower (boots on the ground) is not deployed, the insurgents will eventually win a major military victory. Just as important though, is the need for a meaningful portion of the counterinsurgency forces to come from the local population. If it does not, the counterinsurgency efforts are doomed to failure as well. The use of individuals with local knowledge is just as critical to the military as it is to NGOs as is stated in Brinkerhoff's (2008) work. The insights between these two authors provide a bridge into the domain conflicts discussed by Roberts.

Gregg (2009) ties together many of the concepts in FM 3-24 with those of Galula as well as Max Weber. She points out that the long term goal of counterinsurgency is the building of a functioning state. One of the foundations that must be present is social capital or trust. The use of nonlocal NGOs to rebuild infrastructure is counterproductive. To rebuild social capital, it is more useful to have local Community Development Councils conduct the reconstruction efforts and reach out across ethnic and religious divides to get the projects built. By doing so, the trust that was destroyed by the insurgency and civil strife is rebuilt, allowing governance to begin functioning in a self-sustaining way. This article demonstrates from a different perspective, the domain issues present in the area of international development and some additional pitfalls faced by NGOs attempting to help populations in need.

Nongovernmental Organizations

Brinkerhoff (2008) describes the new actors that have engaged in international development and the boundary conflicts that become evident in practice. This is caused by increasingly aggressive agendas that put these institutions into direct conflict with each other. While the barriers to communications are being overcome in some areas, much more needs to be done to allow these various institutions – the military, civilian government, and NGOs – to work effectively together to achieve the desired goals.

While intervention templates can be helpful to mobilize multi actor responses to crisis, implementation will succeed only if those plans are modified to include local knowledge and to mobilize the commitment of local actors. There are tendencies that need to be avoided: reverting to a view of development management as largely amenable to technical solutions and idealizing and oversimplifying complex societal behaviors and state performance under the good governance rubric. (Brinkerhoff 2008, 987)

This article helps frame the discussion around domain conflicts.

Domain conflict however, does not reside solely between governmental agencies and NGOs. The primary point de Haan (2009) asserts is that donor motives matter - the idea that how much aid is given matters less than how it is given. This ongoing battle between donor motives and the mission of the NGO both within and outside of the organization – and between organizations - creates enormous friction even in benign environments, much less the confused and contested environment of counterinsurgency and stability operations. The motives of the donors as well as the motives of the aid organizations themselves have a stratifying effect on strategies used and how the organizations are perceived both by the target population and other organizations operating in the same domain. The divergent interests of helping the poorest nations versus helping nations that can provide support to the donors' global interests can cause immediate tensions before the aid projects are even out of committee. This is a very insightful text for framing some of the internal issues NGOs face and how it affects their interaction with other agencies. Continuing the further conflicts within the NGO stratum are those that have confounded humanity for eons; religion and ethnicity. Flanigan contends that "FBOs may mirror, reinforce, and reproduce societal divisions that are present in the cultures in which they operate" (2010, p. 3).

Flanigan examines how the same religious identity that provides the impetus for charity and altruism also provides the motivation for violence and hatred. In her study, Flanigan provides critical insights into the behavior patterns of NGOs – particularly the impact religion has on the way NGOs view those they are helping as well as how the NGOs themselves are viewed by the populations they serve. These insights are extremely helpful in building the mosaic of a behavioral template for use in this study. The problem is that not all behaviors exhibited by NGOs and other aid providers are intrinsic to the organizations themselves.

Change Capacity

Layered into this complex and conflicted problem is the backdrop of limited change capacity within the culture these operations are attempting to affect. In the example used for this study, Afghanistan has what is best described as a punctuated equilibrium model for change capacity. The commonality across all disciplines utilizing the punctuated equilibrium model is the concept that deep structure is the key determinant of how a system or organization reacts (Gersick, 1991). The deep structure is the set of choices or initial conditions that determine how the system is organized and what the relationships are between the basic activities that maintain its existence. The deep structure is the force that limits change and maintains equilibrium. Afghan history was reviewed with emphasis placed upon inflection points of cultural change that occurred within the Afghan culture and the drivers of that deep change. Cultural change has occurred primarily in the major cities where the occupying forces established their garrisons. The population in the rural country side have been periodically terrorized and / or raised in revolt but its cultural deep structures have remained unchanged for millennia. The social structure that is at the center of the deep structures is the Afghan Qawm (Miakhel, 2009; Slaughter, 2010). The change capacity of the Qawm is lacking due to the constant tension between the three bases of power from which it derives its identity. When the motors of the punctuated equilibrium change theory entities (Van De Ven & Poole, 1995) are juxtaposed with the power bases, which are the drivers of change within the Qawm, to verify the theory of change at work within the cultural organization, the results are disheartening. The alignment of the change motors with the drivers of change leads to a grounded basis from which to predict a rather limited capacity for change in the Afghan culture. Change initiatives will need to proceed slowly and unfortunately, with the scarcity of resources of the land, they will be very costly to whoever initiates the change effort.

Afghan society is resistant to change by virtue of its long history of conquest, occupation, and paucity of resources (Kakar, 1997; Ewans, 2002; Rasanayagam, 2003; Loyn, 2009). The Afghan culture has evolved to deal with the inability of a central government to provide basic services or even the rule of law. Most rural Afghans think of the central government as a source of interference and corruption (Miakhel, 2009). Police presence in the rural areas is slight if it exists at all. After thirty plus years of occupation and civil war, great portions of the infrastructure were left in ruins. The vast majority of Afghans do not have access to the state-run justice system. Those who do have access typically choose not to use it. Instead, they rely on a mixture of traditional systems (the Jirga), Islamic law, and current power relations to resolve disputes. The outcomes produced by the informal justice system are far from ideal in terms of human rights, but they remain more available, more rapid, and frequently more legitimate, than that of the state system (Miakhel, 2009; Slaughter, 2010).

Throughout its history, Afghanistan has always had a weak central government which caused the development of a strong local level structure. Historically, successful central rulers have worked with clan and religious leaders to achieve balance through compromise (Kakar, 1997; Ewans, 2002; Rasanayagam, 2003; Loyn, 2009). To institute change in Afghan society, the change must be made from the bottom up utilizing the local structures and building consensus. The capacity for radical change is extremely low. Due to the constant state of warfare, the development of both institutions and infrastructure has been stunted and the rural population has been left to fend for itself. This power vacuum was filled by war lords, religious leaders, and clan chieftains that served to keep modernization to a minimum. Change initiatives that are top down in nature and attempt to bypass or ignore tradition and the three power bases will provoke violent rejection. The rejection in the past has meant open rebellion and civil war that has only served to drive the development of the culture and its institution backward in time. The historical record has demonstrated the applicability of the punctuated equilibrium model of change theory. Unfortunately, the record also demonstrates a marked tendency for the constructive motor to drive the society to reorganize around new deep structures that more resemble Hobbes's "state of nature" than a modern contemporary society (Hobbes & Lamprecht, 1949). As Gersick (1991) observes, "This is consistent with the punctuated equilibrium paradigm's implication that systems do not inevitably evolve toward improvement" (p. 31). The Afghan capacity for change is perhaps best described as a thixotropic change capacity model: only slow, deliberate change can be tolerated without causing the fragile bonds that hold the society together to fracture and atomize the organizations and institutions into their component parts. The only way for change to gain ground is to use the libertarian paternalism philosophy of Thaler and Sunstein (2008); always offer choice while trying to positively influence the choice.

CONCLUSION

There have been some fascinating studies on how foreign aid, NGOs, and diplomacy work together (or at odds) in foreign development and national security (Lacquement, 2010). Flanigan (2010) has conducted a study of how NGOs can frequently be very partisan in strife ridden areas causing them to be problematic for cooperative associations with United Nations agencies. Roberts (2010) has conducted a review of where the current state of affairs has progressed. While providing a framework to understand the depth and breadth of the issues involved, the thrust of her work calls for additional research into the appropriate methodologies for dealing with "The Civilian-Military Conundrum in the Post-Cold War Era" (Roberts, 2010, p. 213).

While in some cases, these studies have provided a great depth of information on how NGOs function along with their interaction with the populations they are providing assistance. In other cases there have been very broad surveys of why population centric counterinsurgency operations are a critical capability that should be resident within the Department of Defense (DOD). Sara Lischer has been examining the challenges being faced when integration of NGOs into the planning process in nation building does not take place. Nancy Roberts, a professor of defense analysis at the Naval Postgraduate School in Monterey, has recently published an article lamenting this very issue (Roberts, 2010). Roberts suggest that one of the main issues is the "bleeding boundary" between the military and civilian NGO roles in providing services to distressed populations. From her article, the crux of the issue is the new field manual on Counterinsurgency Operations that has the military displacing the NGOs in the domain of providing humanitarian relief and thereby causing domain consensus to disappear and friction between the groups to escalate.

The problem unfortunately is not as simple as establishing domain consensus. The varieties of NGOs that can be operating in any given area form their own mosaic of goals and intentions. Some of these goals align with those of the interests of the United States – and therefore with the U. S. military – while others may be diametrically opposed. The problem then, for the military commander and other governmental organizations, becomes multifaceted yet the objective remains singular; the population. Even the basic and critical activity of identifying friend from foe, for all organizations involved, becomes complex and constantly shifting. There is a lack of synergy across disciplines in the study of how to establish where the common goals lie and how they can be effectively integrated (Frankie & Guttieri, 2009). Additionally, this integration needs to occur without adversely affecting the ability of each of the organizations involved to operate effectively in accomplishing its goals (Mann, 2008; United States Institute of Peace, (2009); United States Africa Command 2009 Posture Statement).

The scarcity of information available for government policy makers at all levels on the effectiveness of coordinating their missions with those of NGOs present in their area of operations, coupled with a lack of internal expertise, leads to a reduced level of effectiveness in the execution of international intervention. By exploring various options and methods for policy makers to effectively understand how NGOs operate and integrate into the populations they serve, a basic understanding can be established. From this understanding, a robust discussion of integrating both governmental and NGO aid agencies into the planning process can proceed and from there, establish the baseline resource requirements to effectively do so. Additionally, by building simulations for trying different strategies, stability and counterinsurgency operations can be more effectively 'war-gamed' and emergent 'what-ifs' identified. In the complex and crowded space of providing aid to failed or failing nation states, the ability to recognize and experiment with various methods for dealing with domain conflict between the organizations (agents) involved will provide a valuable tool for policy makers and implementers alike.

REFERENCES

Brinkerhoff, D. W. (2008). The state and international development management: Shifting tides, changing boundaries, and future directions. *Public Administration Review*, *68*(November), 985–1001. doi:10.1111/j.1540-6210.2008.00948.x

de Haan, A. (2009). *How the aid industry works: An introduction to international development*. Sterling, VA: Kumarian Press.

Ewans, M. (2002). *Afghanistan*. New York: HarperCollins Publishers, Inc.

Flanigan, S. (2010). *For the love of god: NGOS and religious identity in a violent world*. Sterling, VA: Kumarian Press.

FM 3-24 The Army / Marine Corps Field Manual on Counterinsurgency. (2006). Retrieved February 4, 2011, from www.fas.org/irp/doddir/army/fm3-24.pdf

Franke, V. C., & Guttieri, K. (2009). Picking up the pieces: Are United States officers ready for nation building? *Journal of Political and Military Sociology*, *37*(1), 1–25.

Galula, D. (1964). *Counterinsurgency warfare: Theory and Practice. Forward by John A. Nagl. 2006.* Westport, CT: Praeger Security International.

Gentile, G. P. (2009). A strategy of tactics: Population-centric COIN and the Army. *Parameters, 3*(Autumn), 5–17.

Gersick, C. J. (1991). Revolutionary change theories: A multilevel exploration of the punctuated equilibrium paradigm. *Academy of Management Review, 16*(1), 10–36. doi:10.5465/AMR.1991.4278988

Gleick, J. (1988). *Chaos: The making of a new science.* New York: Penguin Books.

Goode, S. M. (2009). A historical basis for force requirements in counterinsurgency. *Parameters, 4*(Winter), 45–57.

Gregg, H. S. (2009). Beyond population engagement: Understanding counterinsurgency. *Parameters, 3*(Autumn), 18–30.

Hobbes, T., & Lamprecht, S. P. (1949). *De Cive: Or, the Citizen.* New York: Appleton-Century-Crofts.

Kakar, M. H. (1997). *Afghanistan: The Soviet invasion and the Afghan response, 1979-1982.* Berkeley, CA: University of California Press.

Lacquement, R. A. (2010). Integrating civilian and military activities. *Parameters, 1*(Spring), 20–33.

Lischer, S. K. (2007). Military intervention and the "force multiplier.". *Global Governance, 13*, 99–118.

Loyn, D. (2009). *In Afghanistan.* New York: Palgrave Macmillan.

Mann, S. (2008). Taking Interagency Stability Operations to a New Level: The Integration of Special Operation Forces and USAID in Afghanistan. *Small Wars Journal.* Retrieved June 19, 2010, from http://smallwarsjournal.com/documents/79-mann.pdf

Miakhel, S. (2009). *Understanding Afghanistan: The importance of tribal culture and structure in security and governance.* Pashtoonkhwa. Retrieved July 2, 2011, from http://www.pashtoonkhwa.com/files/books/Miakhel-ImportanceOfTribalStructuresInAfghanistan.pdf

Nagl, J. A. (2005). *Counterinsurgency Lessons from Malaya and Vietnam.* Chicago, IL: The University of Chicago Press.

Nagl, J. A. (2006). *Forward to Counterinsurgency warfare: Theory and Practice, by David Galula*. Westport, CT: Praeger Security International.

Portes, A. (2010). *Economic sociology: A systematic Inquiry*. Princeton, NJ: Princeton University Press. doi:10.1515/9781400835171

Rasanayagam, A. (2003). *Afghanistan: A modern history*. London: I. B. Tauris and Company, LTD.

Roberts, N. C. (2010). Spanning bleeding boundaries: Humanitarianism, NGOs, and the civilian-military nexus in the post-cold war era. *Public Administration Review, 70*(March), 212–222. doi:10.1111/j.1540-6210.2010.02135_2.x

Slaughter, S. R. (2010). *Expanding the Qawm: Culturally savvy counterinsurgency and nation-building in Afghanistan. Monograph*. Fort Leavenworth, KS: School of Advanced Military Studies, United States Army Command and General Staff College.

Snow, D. M. (1993). *Peacekeeping, peacemaking and peace-enforcement: The U.S. role in the new international order*. Carlisle Barracks, PA: Strategic Studies Institute, U.S. Army War College.

Stremlau, J. (1998). *People in Peril: Human Rights, Humanitarian Action, and Preventing Deadly Conflict*. Washington, DC: Carnegie Corporation of New York.

Thaler, R. H., & Sunstein, C. R. (2008). *Nudge: Improving decisions about health, wealth, and happiness*. New Haven, CT: Yale University Press.

United Nations General Assembly Resolution 46/182. (1992). *Strengthening of the coordination of humanitarian emergency assistance of the United Nations: Guiding principles*. New York: United Nations.

United Nations General Assembly Resolution 52/167. (1998). *Safety and security of humanitarian personnel*. New York: United Nations.

United States Africa Command 2009 Posture Statement. (n.d.). Retrieved February 4, 2011, from www.africom.mil/pdfFiles/USAFRICOM2009PostureStatement.pdf

United States Central Intelligence Agency. (2012). *The World Factbook*. Retrieved February 9, 2012, from https://www.cia.gov/library/publications/resources/the-world-factbook/

United States Institute of Peace and Peacekeeping. (2009). *Guiding principles for stabilization and reconstruction*. Washington, DC: Author.

Valentino, B. A. (2011). The true cost of humanitarian intervention: The hard truth about a noble notion. *Foreign Affairs*, *90*(6), 60–73.

Van de Ven, A. H., & Poole, M. S. (1995). Explaining development and change in organizations. *Academy of Management Review*, *20*(3), 510–540. doi:10.2307/258786

KEY TERMS AND DEFINITIONS

Complex Humanitarian Interventions: These operations run the gambit from humanitarian relief such as food delivery, to full scale warfare conducted on the behalf of one of the belligerents.

Counterinsurgency Operations: Military and civil operations conducted to win the support of the population to stop or nullify the efforts of a counter-government movement.

Humanitarian Relief: Operations that typically follow natural disasters such as food and medical aid deliveries.

Nongovernmental Organizations: These organizations operate independently of governments and conduct operations in accordance with their 'mission.' These organizations can be religious (faith based) or nonsectarian, and they may or may not be willing to coordinate their actions with those of government entities (particularly the military).

Peace Enforcement: The separation of belligerents and enforcement of a ceasefire through the use of armed military forces. The key difference between peace enforcement and peace keeping is that one or more of the belligerents has not agreed to the terms and will return to open hostilities given the opportunity.

Peace Keeping: The monitoring of the separation and ceasefire agreed to by the belligerents in a conflict.

Warfare: Open and unrestricted conflict.

Chapter 2
Literature Review

INTRODUCTION

Pacification, nation building, stability operations, counterinsurgency operations – these are all various names for the activities a victorious military force finds itself undertaking at the cessation of hostilities. This is especially true of the belligerents in a civil war. The international community steps in in an effort to contain the hostilities and deliver humanitarian aid to the refugee population that is inevitably created by the hostilities. Frequently the outcome of a war cannot truly be known for several years after the guns have fallen silent. Does the defeated state rebuild its capacity for governance and join with its former antagonist in peaceful and mutually prosperous relations or does it descend into the Hobbesian hell of a failed nation state; a pariah to the world community? There have been examples of errors made by victors, such as the Treaty of Versailles, that have set the stage for future conflicts that have lessons applicable to humanitarian interventions initiated by the international community.

BACKGROUND

A lack of empathy, driven by greed, hubris, or lack of cultural understanding can lead to Tuchman's (1969) definition of folly. The different approaches, one approach showing empathy and a respect for the change capacity of a vanquished foe, the other showing the opposite, can be found in the handling

DOI: 10.4018/978-1-5225-1782-5.ch002

of Germany in the twentieth century. The vengeful stance that the Allies took with Germany after World War I is frequently cited as the casus belli for World War II by setting the conditions that allowed Hitler's rise to power (Van Meter, 1979). But then after World War II, Germany (at least West Germany) had a completely different outcome.

The historic postwar transition effects on societies have been almost as traumatic as the lethal portion of the battles themselves. At the end of World War I, the victorious Allies came together at Versailles Palace in Paris to hammer out a peace treaty, the Treaty of Versailles. The treaty has historically been seen as a disaster as far as actually making peace. Given the costs paid by the Allies, both in blood and treasure and the mood of their respective electorates, the ability of the 'Big Three' democracies, Britain, France, and the United States, to make peace based upon reciprocity, was very low. The United States had the additional difficulty that isolationism was a very strong sentiment during that time. So much of an isolationist sentiment was present that the United States never ratified the Treaty of Versailles or became a member of the League of Nations (Dockrill & Fisher, 2001).

The case of Germany after World War II was quite different than that existing after World War I. The main difference in the situation on the ground was that the Allies had invaded and were occupying Germany. Much of the German infrastructure had been destroyed and resources were scarce. Many members of the disarmed German army were attempting to be captured by the Allied forces because prisoners of war were allotted the same rations as Allied soldiers, which was much better than the civilian population were able to attain. There were also a great number of displaced persons and disbanded German army personnel (still under arms) walking around the countryside making for an uncomfortable security situation. The positive aspect of the security situation was that none of these worrisome groups were organizing into an insurgency. The main problem faced by the Allied occupation forces was crime and reestablishing civil order. Unfortunately, one of the situations that remained the same between the wars was the propensity of the United States to rapidly withdraw manpower assets from the theater due to the rapid demobilization of its military. This made the security circumstances then, as it has in the recent past, problematic for commanders attempting to conduct stability operations (United States Army History Archives, 1947).

Fortunately for many of the German people, the strife between the Soviet Union and the other Allies became an overriding consideration in the administration of postwar Germany. The fear of communism spreading coupled with the insistence of building a buffer zone by the Soviet Union at the end of the war begat the Marshall Plan for rebuilding postwar Europe. As the perceived threat from the Soviet Union grew, the punishment of Germany took a backseat to the need to rebuild the Allied areas of control to keep Germany from falling completely under the control of the Soviet Union. The military occupation administration of government, wanting to turn over governance in the Allied occupied areas as rapidly as possible, took on an increasing level of reciprocity in its outlook. This desired outcome was not a grand reach for German society. The battle that was taking place was one over the type of governance that would replace fascism. Rule of law, property rights, and an industrial economic base already existed. This helps to demonstrate the success that can follow from maintaining end state goals within the change capacity of the targeted society.

MAIN FOCUS OF THE CHAPTER

The previous outcomes were brought about by nation states exerting their influence in a purely governmental fashion. Nongovernmental organizations played only a minor role in the overall outcome of transition operations. The emergence of nongovernmental organizations as actors in the delivery of humanitarian goods and services in the aftermath of combat brings an additional variable into policy consideration. The public-private dichotomy of relief aid for displaced non-combatants causes friction to develop between the two sectors. This leads to what Roberts (2010) describes as what happened when the United States military began forming Provincial Reconstruction Teams (PRTs). When these PRTs, consisting of military and civilian personnel from various U.S. Government agencies, specialists in the social and economic sciences as well as developmental specialists, began interacting with the local and regional political leaders by sponsoring civil engagement and reconstruction activities, a series of domain questions arose. Roberts also contends that the hierarchical methods of working top down have not proven effective in the field. Further complicating transitions from war to peace are the motives and efforts that humanitarian nongovernmental organizations play when they enter the area to provide relief for the beleaguered civilian populace that has been exposed to the ravages of war.

The aid process is fraught with challenges and problems that are as resistant to solution as the conditions they hope to ameliorate. Humanitarian aid is rarely neutral or is it perceived as neutral even when it is delivered with that intention. When aid is delivered to refugees in a conflict, it can be perceived as a hostile act by the opposing belligerents. This is because the delivery of aid can enable the continuation or even broadening of hostilities. Lischer

(2007) points to the delivery of aid to Afghan refugees in Pakistan during the Soviet occupation of the country as a case in point. In her view, the same has held true in other humanitarian operations throughout the past thirty years of international activism: "Relying on a purely humanitarian response to civil war and genocide is an ineffective and potentially harmful placebo" (Lischer, 2007, p. 114). In *A Fragile Balance*, Picard and Buss (2009) provide a history of foreign aid through the lens that current foreign aid practices have lost their alignment and focus. They hold that foreign aid can best be used to provide social services and develop human resources but it is not an effective tool to promote economic growth - which is the lack of alignment and focus they see in current situations. When aid is provided injudiciously for the development of democracy and governance, the exact opposite can occur by fostering political instability through the monetary support of opposition political parties. Unfortunately, there has been an ever increasing appetite for such aid in the United States since the end of the cold war.

Dennis Young asks if the relationship between non-profit organizations and the United States government is "complementary, supplementary, or adversarial?" (Young, 2006, p. 37). He answers the question in the affirmative with the caveat that the relationship will vary among the three depending on the circumstances. The relationship becomes even more dynamic where foreign assistance is involved. There has been an historic tendency for the United States to utilize foreign aid as an instrument of national policy. From the 'cold war' to the 'war on terror' after 9/11, the money from USAID does not necessarily go to the neediest countries, it goes to strategic allies. As an example, in 2004 Egypt and Israel received $13 and $121 per capita respectively in assistance where Bangladesh and Ghana each received only $3 per capita (Kerlin, 2006).

There are several tools available to various coalition policy makers for achieving policy goals. In addition to foreign aid the tools include:

- Threat and use of force
- Covert operations and proxy interventions
- Intelligence gathering and information dissemination
- Diplomacy
- Propaganda
- Cultural exchanges (visits and exchanges)
- Economic threats and promises and trade policies (sanctions and tariffs). (Picard & Buss, 2009, p. 6)

Each of these tools provides for varying degrees of cooperation between NGOs and the United Nations. In the supplemental role, NGOs and international government agencies perform separate but parallel roles in helping a population. In the complementary role, the NGOs and international governmental agencies coordinate closely with each other in the provision of goods and services to the targeted population; each providing strength where the other may struggle (Young, 2006).

Policy makers need an understanding of various aid organizations' strategies and likely behaviors to enable accurate assessments of potential interactions and their outcomes in the execution of transition and stability operations. Crutchfield and Grant (2008) describe the six successful practices of non-profit organizations. The practices they describe that make these organizations successful also make them formidable to deal with in the delivery of development aid in failed and failing nation states. Those six practices are:

1. **They Advocate and Serve:** They work to deliver services as well as advocate for policy initiatives.
2. **They Make Markets Work:** They tap into the economic self-interests of the parties in populations they work in.
3. **They Inspire Evangelists:** From both within and without of the populations they serve to cement their advocacy within society.
4. **They Nurture Nonprofit Networks:** Which is in keeping with the axiom that a rising tide lifts all ships.
5. **They Master the Art of Adaptation:** They learn to innovate to keep themselves relevant.
6. **They Share Leadership:** By power sharing, these organizations empower their succession plans and provide a gateway for individuals to advance within the organization. (Crutchfield & Grant, 2008, pp. 21-22)

These practices and skills can become an inherent source of tension when these types of organizations attempt to deliver services in a counterinsurgency environment. The advocacy piece of their mission can, and frequently does, lead to conflict in the delivery of development aid in a contested environment and has a ripple effect on policy implementation (Leed & Taylor, 2010).

The idea of the population's trust being the prize is not limited to operations involving the use of military security forces. Much of the development aid taking place in the developing world fights to gain the trust of the indigenous societies where the aid is being expended (Mosse, 2005). This ongoing battle creates enormous friction even in benign environments, much less the confused and contested environment of counterinsurgency and stability operations. The motives of the donors as well as the motives of the aid organizations themselves have a stratifying effect on strategies used and how the organizations are perceived both by the target population and other organizations operating in the same domain (de Haan, 2009).

The domain conflicts become even more pronounced when military forces are introduced (Roberts, 2010). There is a definite tension about which organization has the right to operate in a particular domain space in the area. As the threat level increases and domain consensus decreases, the strife between the various aid agencies and the military reach their greatest. Figure 1 depicts the various military activities that have interaction with NGOs and various aid organizations and the relative degree of domain consensus associated with each (Roberts, 2010). The upper quadrants represent high levels of domain consensus. Each of the agents is operating within their traditional space and the friction between the groups is greatly reduced. In fact, there has been a traditionally high level of trust and cooperation in disaster relief operations when the military is providing logistics support to NGOs and other government sponsored aid agencies. The threat level is high for disaster relief because the situation will have typically overwhelmed the NGO's and receiving government's ability to effectively respond. This cooperation is reversed when counterinsurgency operations are begun by the military and / or complex humanitarian missions are begun such as those in Darfur.

The phrase "winning hearts and minds" is usually credited to the writing of Galula (1964). His work on counterinsurgency warfare is one of the prime references cited in the Army / Marine Corps field manual on Counterinsurgency Opreations, FM 3-24. Galula writes from a mechanistic and ethically neutral perspective in that he describes in very calculating terms how to turn a population against an insurgent, thereby destroying the insurgents' source of power. He identifies the center of gravity (the origin of the belligerents' source of power) for both the insurgent and the counterinsurgent as the population itself. From his perspective, protecting the population from harm is not an act of humanity; it is an act of expediency. The battle is joined literally to win over the goodwill of the population. The degree of intelligence, or information, about the insurgents' activities that is forthcoming from the population, is the scorecard of measure. His capstone argument is that if the population feels more secure by cooperating with the counterinsurgent forces, then the insurgent has lost and can be relatively quickly eradicated from the scene. On the other hand, if the population lives in fear of the insurgents' reprisal for cooperating with the counterinsurgent forces (or the established local government agencies), then the counterinsurgent forces are condemned to chasing shadows in a self-defeating effort to counter idealism

Figure 1. Domain concensus

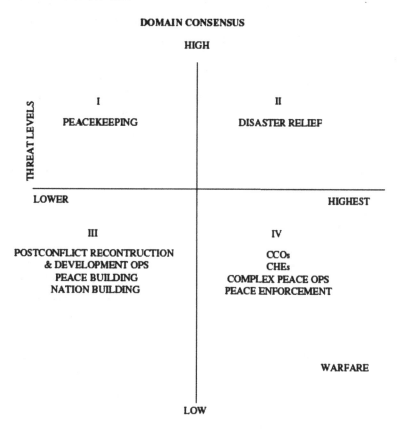

with kinetic force (Galula, 1964). The lesson that has been taken from this by many military planners is that humanitarian operations can act as a force multiplier; a way to increase security without the use of force. Lischer (2007) adamantly refutes this position and contends that it has precisely the opposite effect.

FM 3-24 is basically a synthesis of these two concepts represented by the previously discussed texts. The field manual discusses at length the need to provide security for the population and to insulate the population from the insurgents. Additionally, FM 7-0 discusses the various levels of conventional force versus facilitation in the full spectrum of possible military operations. There is a great deal of emphasis put on the importance of constant learning and studying the 'lessons learned' from predecessors operating in the area. Centralized command and decentralized execution is the watch phrase for counterinsurgent operations with the protection of the population the foremost mission. The introduction of political officials and social workers down to the company level is a drastic departure from previous military doctrine (Gentile, 2009). (While this structure is advocated in doctrine, current force structure levels do not accommodate such experts below the level of the division – fully four levels above where doctrine says they are needed.) The field manual has adopted tactics that Mao would have felt very comfortable with in the Chinese 'Long March.' Unfortunately, in this new perspective that U.S. forces now see aid provision sets the views of NGOs in direct opposition. The one organization that has the influence and moral authority to intervene and coordinate the activities of each is the United Nations High Commissioner for Refugees (UNHCR). Unfortunately, this office is a reluctant intermediary (Lischer, 2005).

Change Capacity

As discussed earlier, the change capacity of a society has a clear and direct bearing on what end states are feasible when planning for and executing stability operations and humanitarian interventions. Van De Ven and Poole (1995) identify four families of ideal-type theories of social change. Those families are life cycle, evolution, dialectic, and teleology. The authors identify a great number of traits in the ideal-types of theories of social change. In the ideal-type of evolution, they identify the key metaphor being competitive survival and the generating force being population scarcity, competition, and commensalism (Van De Ven & Poole, 1995). Of the four ideal-types, evolution is the one that has traits that are the most similar to those that also occur in the circumstances surrounding Afghan culture.

Gersick (1991) also makes the comparison of the traditional paradigm of gradual blending of small changes to make a different form, to that of punctuated equilibrium, which has long periods of stability punctuated by radical change. Gersick asserts that the "Darwinian gradualism" type models that apply drivers such as efficiency, constantly moving a system forward, are frequently fallacious (Gersick, 1991, p. 10). Punctuated equilibria do not have a smooth or constant path toward pre-set ends; the very definition of the system can be modified by its evolution. The article describes "the three main components of the punctuated equilibrium paradigm: deep structure, equilibrium periods, and revolutionary periods" (Gersick, 1991, p. 13).

Common across all disciplines utilizing the punctuated equilibrium model is the concept that deep structure is the key determinant of how a system or organization reacts. The deep structure is the set of choices or initial conditions that determine how the system is organized and what the relationships are between the basic activities that maintain its existence. The deep structure is the force that limits change and maintains equilibrium. It is only "when a system's deep structure comes apart" that revolutionary change occurs, which "may not leave a system better off" (Gersick, 1991, p. 20). Gersick (1991) suggests that there can be numerous triggers for revolutionary periods; both internal and external. An example of an external trigger would be the need to obtain resources from the environment and using inappropriate tools to do so. An internal trigger could be temporal milestones such as the half way point of a project (Gersick, 1991, p. 24). Individuals in their forties, having reached the half way point in their lives, frequently will make dramatic changes in their lifestyle in an effort to optimize the remaining period of productive time they have left to them (Gersick, 1991, p. 24). In all of these examples however, turbulence in the system can mask the inertia present in the deep structures.

Afghan Geography and History

The geography and history of Afghanistan has done more to influence the culture of the people than any other single influence (Kakar, 1997; Ewans, 2002; Rasanayagam, 2003; Loyn, 2009). Afghanistan is a landlocked country covering approximately 250,000 square miles, which is an area roughly the size of the state of Texas (Ewans, 2002). The country's location on the eastern end of the Iranian Plateau has given it a central place in trade between East and West for several millennia. As far back 1336 BC, a ship carrying lapis lazuli and tin mined in Afghanistan was wrecked off the Turkish coast (Ewans, 2002, p. 10). The location of Afghanistan has also given it a reputation as a highway of conquest.

The climate of the country can be extreme. Over two-thirds of the country lies over 5,000 feet in elevation and it harbors several of the highest mountain peaks in the world (Ewans, 2002, p. 1). Because of its landlocked location, rainfall is light and water is scarce. Large diurnal and seasonal swings in temperature make agriculture difficult. The majority of the land is uncultivable but the snowmelt fed rivers lend themselves to irrigation. Small land holdings are the norm which has prevented many of the extremes of hunger and malnutrition seen in many other parts of Asia (Ewans, 2002). The majority of the almost 30 million people (The CIA World Fact Book estimate) subsist on agriculture and pastoralism. Most of the arable land is used in the production of food grains, but there are some important cash crops such as cotton, fruit, and ever present opium (Ewans, 2002, p. 3).

The location of Afghanistan also holds the key to the diversity of its people. Afghanistan borders Iran, Turkmenistan, Uzbekistan, Tajikistan, China, and

Pakistan. The majority of the population is ethnic Pashtun, which are of Indo-Aryan decent, and refer to themselves as collectively as Afghans and their language as Afghani (Ewans, 2002, pp. 4 -5). The Pashtun language is one of the Indo-Iranian groups and is related to Persian. The ethnic makeup of the Afghan population is as follows from the CIA World Fact Book 2011: Pashtun forty-two percent, Tajik twenty-seven percent, Hazara nine percent, Uzbek nine percent, Aimak four percent, Turkmen three percent, Baloch two percent, and other four percent. Most all of these ethnic groups have emigrated from neighboring countries primarily as a result of conquest.

Conquest has been a way of life in the modern history of Afghanistan. During the Seventh Century the Arab Caliphates extended into Afghanistan. This advancement of Islam into previously held Hindu lands established what would be the battleground between Western and Eastern influences (Ewans, 2002). One of the most devastating events in Afghan history is the invasion of the Mongol hordes commanded by Genghis Khan in 1221 (Ewans, 2002). The result of the Mongol occupation of Afghanistan was devastating on the population. Entire city populations were shattered. Visitors were informed that the entirety of the "citizens had been removed" (Ewans, 2002, p. 24).

In the late 1830's the one invasion route that was certain in British eyes was that of Russia and Persia crossing through Afghanistan to invade India. The British' fear that Afghanistan would be used as an invasion route of India was not without historic precedence and led them to invade Afghanistan to utilize it as a buffer. There were two Anglo-Afghan wars or more accurately British interventions. From 1838 to 1842, the British supported Shah Shuja, who they installed as the ruler of Afghanistan, with an army of 20,000 soldiers (Ewans, 2002; Rasanayagam, 2003; Loyn, 2009). The first intervention came to an end when, after a series of military and political mistakes and missteps, the remaining British army retreated to Jalalabad. The retreat was conducted through narrow mountain passes during harsh winter conditions while suffering continuous ambushes from local tribesmen in the surrounding hills. The result was a death march in which nearly all of the 9,500 British-Indian troops and 12,000 Indian camp followers died (Ewans, 2002; Rasanayagam, 2003; Loyn, 2009).

The second foray by the British into Afghanistan in 1879 went little better than the first. After a hasty declaration of war, the British invaded Afghanistan and quickly dispersed the defenders. Unfortunately, they soon discovered a glaring problem; they had no popular figure to rule Afghanistan. The cost of keeping an occupying army garrisoned was not planned for and would be a serious drain on the Exchequer in India. The current Amir was the "less-than-favorite son" (Ewans, 2002, p. 88) of a man that had successfully ruled Afghanistan in the preceding 10 years. This set of circumstances left the British with little choice but to make terms with the new Amir, but the peace was short lived. The Amir was not powerful enough to control all of the tribes and a mere six weeks after the terms were agreed to, the British envoy and his small contingent of cavalry were killed by a mob. The British response was brutal and prompted the Afghans to come together to fight a jihad. Although the British prevailed militarily, they were again faced with a long occupation which the government in London had no stomach for. A new Amir was allowed to come to power and the British retired from Afghanistan again within a year (Ewans, 2002; Rasanayagam, 2003; Loyn, 2009).

Just as the Afghans were caught in the struggles of the imperialist powers of the nineteenth century, they were caught in the Cold War rivalries in the twentieth century. As the United States lost Iran, its ally and partner in the region, to Islamic revolution, the Soviet Union began to have concerns about American interests in Afghanistan (Ewans, 2002; Rasanayagam, 2003; Loyn, 2009). In 1978, a coup took place that installed a decisively left leaning government. The People's Democratic Party of Afghanistan (PDPA) took power and began to try to bring Afghanistan from a feudal state to a socialist one (Kakar, 1997). With revolutionary zeal, the PDPA faithful spread out into the countryside to attempt land reform. Through a combination of poor planning and poor knowledge of local traditions in the countryside, land reform was a failure and provoked opposition to the new government and sowed the seeds of unrest that would eventually spark the Soviet invasion of the country in 1979.

The Soviet invasion and installation of puppet government was no more successful than the British efforts a century earlier. The Soviets left Afghanistan with a relatively small number of almost 15,000 dead but an astounding 469,685 casualties, out of a force of 642,000 personnel that served during their ten year occupation (Grau, 1996, p. xvi). After these ten years of occupation, Afghanistan had once again shed the yoke of occupation only to bear the new one of civil war. In 1996 the Taliban began to consolidate power and extend its influence over the majority of the country. Initially supported by Pakistan, the Taliban proved to be an unreliable ally. They set up what for all practical purposes was a theocracy based on ultra conservative Islamic beliefs (Fuller, 1991). Unfortunately, they did not address rebuilding of the country's infrastructure and effectively dismantled the administrative bureaucracy. During their five years in power, Afghanistan further disintegrated into a failed state with a paucity of resources and a devastated infrastructure. It has become a rentier state dependent upon development aid (Rasanayagam, 2003). The story of how the International Community will fair in attempting to modernize Afghanistan is still being written but historic precedent does not suggest a successful outcome.

The culture of the Pashtuns has been shaped by the history of conquest of the region (Rasanayagam, 2003; Loyn, 2009). They are a proud people that are aggressively individualistic in the context of a tribal and familial culture (Ewans, 2002). The Pashtun have predatory habits blended with a mix of democratic and feudal ethos which is vetted through a relatively simple code of conduct reinforced by their Muslim faith. Concepts of revenge (badal), hospitality (melmastia) sanctuary, and honor (namus) have meant that vendettas have gone on for generations and the lack of any firm rules of succession only add to internal factionalism (Ewans, 2002; Miakhel, 2009).

The recent past is littered with the dashed agendas of those that attempted deep change in Afghanistan. During the reign of King Amanullah Khan (1919-1929), he attempted to implement reform agendas to modernize Afghanistan but met resistance from both religious leaders and the clans. He could not find the proper balance between the three bases of power and was forced to abdicate his throne and leave the country. When Afghan President Daud (1973-1978), focused on implementing a progressive nationalistic agenda he was overthrown by a Communist coup supported by Islamic fundamentalists that feared he was becoming too close to the West (Kakar, 1997). Jihad started against the communist regimes (1978-1992) when their policies began to target religious and Khel leaders, and they failed to implement their agenda. The Taliban lost power when they began bypassing Khel leaders with their agenda and plunged the country into civil war (Ewans, 2002; Rasanayagam, 2003; Loyn, 2009; Miakhel, 2009).

The Qawm

Up until 2002, Afghanistan continued to be a feudal type of government in which the tribes held a critical role in installing and removing their rulers. They were also critical in keeping order and providing governance in the rural countryside where central government power was low if even present at all (Miakhel, 2009). With the marginalization of the central government throughout a history of conquest, rebellion, and civil war, the Afghans have adapted their traditional system of governance to exercise the rule of law at the local level within their fragmented society. Their traditional system of an almost ubiquitous code of conduct called pashtunwali provides a system of rules and expectations to govern life for Afghans. This system is reinforced by the egalitarian nature of Afghan society (for male heads of households) which gives adult males a vote in local decision making (Slaughter, 2010).

This discussion of tribes however, should not be construed as having described the cultural source of identity for Afghans. In fact, Dupree (1973) points out that tribe "has, in general, degenerated into a term of identification when away from one's own village or area" (p. 183). Slaughter (2010) points out that the "The Pashtun tribe is not hierarchical and there is no chief, single man, or office that speaks for the Pashtun tribe or some sub-division thereof" (p. 7). The other ethno-linguistic groups frequently identified as tribes in Afghanistan are not tribes at all. This makes the notion of tribe almost useless in terms of analytical value (Tapper, 1983). The true source of identity for Afghans comes from the notion of the Qawm (Miakhel, 2009).

The term Qawm can be roughly interpreted to mean "social network" (Miakhel, 2009, p. 2). It is from this social network that Afghans have drawn their social capital to be able to bounce back from the repeated insults of occupation, civil war, famine, and failed governance. This concept of social capital is in line with the forms of capital described by Pierre Bourdieu (2010): social capital, made up of social obligations ('connections'), which is convertible, in certain conditions, into economic capital" (p. 281). This point is a regular feature expected of Afghan leaders. The Qawm chooses leaders or Khans based upon the expectation that they will be good providers (Slaughter, 2010). So the Qawm may best be described to the Western way of thinking as an über political party, replete with expectations of patronage and the sense of loyalty to the Qawm derived from that patronage. In Afghanistan, the Qawm has provided security and order during times of chaos but has also been the culprit of preventing the modernization of the nation (Miakhel, 2009). The Qawm derives its authority based upon the three bases of identity and power in Afghanistan: the Khel, Islam, and the central government. The Khel is a combination of three attributes: the location where a man lives, his method of livelihood, and his clan or extended family.

Islam is of fundamental importance in Afghan culture and has a dominant influence on the way individuals view the world. Madrassas are the religious schools that produce clerics. There are official Madrassas, supported by the government and non-official Madrassas, supported by contributions from individuals and organizations. The non-official Madrassas are usually located in mosques and therefore closer to the community. Leaders from the non-official Madrassas can mobilize the community very easily because they live among the people and are supported by the community. Lessening the status of graduates of official Madrassas is that many of them are appointed as judges and prosecutors and because of the rampant corruption in the judicial system, viewed by the people as corrupt officials. The central government is frequently looked at as an outside interference that is inherently corrupt (Miakhel, 2009).

Figure 2 illustrates the relationships that make up the Qawm. The interests for the individual, based in the Qawm, are the meeting or balance point of the tensions between these three power bases. As one power base gains power, it begins to shift the relationship of the Qawm with the other two. However, this shifting of relationships has a thixotropic quality. This is because the bonds within the Afghan society are tenuous at best. Independence and individualism, as well as a very inflated value placed on honor can cause what appear to be solid organizations to atomize (Ewans, 2002; Rasanayagam, 2003; Loyn, 2009; Miakhel, 2009).

If the changes of relationship between the power bases occur with enough temporal space, the transitions take place with little resistance. If change is too rapid or too much force is used, the capacity for change becomes brittle and shatters the power base from which the change effort was launched, devastating the effort. The Khel and Islam act as the prescriptive motors that drive the adaptive change process. The central government acts as the constructive motor that attempts to drive transformative change in the society

Figure 2. The Nexus of Power is the Qawm

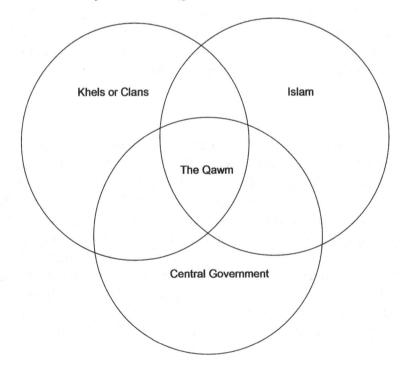

and get it to re-coalesce around new modern deep structures (Tushman & Romanelli, 1985; Van De Ven & Poole, 1995). Unfortunately, those attempts have generally led to revolt, civil war, and the degeneration of the country into a mid-evil society (Kakar, 1997).

With this in mind, there are two other concepts that are critical to the understanding of the Afghan way. In the preponderance of the countryside there are locally established structures to administer justice. The Jirga is a consensus building forum for making decisions. It is a "gathering of representatives of tribes or of different segments of the society" (Miakhel, 2009, p. 8). The Shura is a council that is elected to act for longer periods of time. In Afghan rural culture, unilateral decisions may not be implemented – either a Jirga or a Shura is convened to conduct the decision making process and their decisions have the weight of law (Miakhel, 2009; Slaughter, 2010). Interestingly, the Jirgas are assembled in an ad hoc fashion and only with the acquiescence of the disputing parties much like a jury is selected in the United States justice system – the members can and do change for each issue. If the belligerent sides cannot agree on the members of the Jirga, then the Jirga cannot be held. The Jirga bases its decisions on precedent which is called Narkh which is essentially common law in the Western sense (Miakhel, 2009).

Given the supremacy of the existing local cultural structures within Afghan society, the failure of both internal and external change imperatives should be expected. The fragmented nature of Afghan culture combined with its traditional and conservative leanings stand as a formidable barrier to modernization efforts. Change initiatives must proceed slowly and unfortunately, with the paucity of resources of the land, they will be very costly to whoever initiates the change effort.

CONCLUSION

The dynamics of these complex adaptive systems are rooted in their deep structure. The deep structure is the grouping of organizing choices or variables that determine the system's basic activity patterns (Gersick, 1991). The broad nature of the literature reviewed was necessary to provide the background regarding the interrelationships between the various theories of inputs and outcomes and their sometimes-disjointed actual outcomes in reality. Lischer (2005) has pointed out that when NGOs or a military force attempt to deal with complex humanitarian problems independently, they frequently wind up making the problem worse. She cites multiple examples from Afghanistan to Darfur to the Balkans where NGOs operating independently actually facilitated the spread of a conflict. She also cites examples of military forces exacerbating problems in Iraq, Afghanistan, and the Balkans as well. Issues ranging from military-NGO coordination to change capacity of the society as well as the legitimacy of the belligerents within the society are captured within this simulation and provide the context for the interpretation of the results of the simulations.

REFERENCES

Berry, B. J. L., Kiel, L. D., & Elliott, E. (2002). Adaptive agents, intelligence, and emergent human organization: Capturing complexity through agent based modeling. *Proceedings of the National Academy of Sciences of the United States of America, 99*(S3), 7187-7316.

Bourdieu, P. (2010). The forms of capital. In N. W. Biggart (Ed.), *Readings in economic sociology* (pp. 280–291). Malden, MA: Blackwell Publishers Inc.

Crutchfield, L. R., & Grant, H. M. (2008). *Forces for good: The six practices of high-impact nonprofits*. San Francisco, CA: Jossey-Bass.

de Haan, A. (2009). *How the aid industry works: An introduction to international development*. Sterling, VA: Kumarian Press.

Dockrill, M. L., & Fisher, J. (2001). *The Paris Peace Conference, 1919: Peace without victory?* New York, NY: Palgrave.

Dupree, L. (1973). *Afghanistan*. Oxford, UK: Oxford University Press.

Epstein, J. M., & Axtell, R. (1996). *Growing artificial societies: Social science from the bottom up*. Washington, DC: Brookings Institution Press.

Ewans, M. (2002). *Afghanistan*. New York: HarperCollins Publishers, Inc.

FM 3-24 The Army / Marine Corps Field Manual on Counterinsurgency. (2006). Retrieved February 4, 2011, from www.fas.org/irp/doddir/army/fm3-24.pdf

FM 7-0 The Army Field Manual on Training for Full Spectrum Operations. (2008). Retrieved June 19, 2010, from http://usacac.army.mil/cac2/Repository/FM70/FM7-0.pdf

Fuller, G. E. (1991). *Islamic fundamentalism in Afghanistan: Its character and prospects*. Santa Monica, CA: Rand.

Galula, D. (1964). *Counterinsurgency warfare: Theory and Practice.* Westport, CT: Praeger Security International.

Gentile, G. P. (2009). A strategy of tactics: Population-centric COIN and the Army. *Parameters*, *3*(Autumn), 5–17.

Gersick, C. J. (1991). Revolutionary change theories: A multilevel exploration of the punctuated equilibrium paradigm. *Academy of Management Review*, *16*(1), 10–36. doi:10.5465/AMR.1991.4278988

Grau, L. W. (1996). *The bear went over the mountain: Soviet combat tactics in Afghanistan.* Washington, DC: National Defense University Press.

Kakar, M. H. (1997). *Afghanistan: the Soviet invasion and the Afghan response, 1979-1982.* Berkeley, CA: University of California Press.

Kerlin, J. (2006). U.S. based international NGOs and federal government foreign assistance: Out of Alignment? In E. T. Boris & C. E. Steuerle (Eds.), *Nonprofits and government: Collaboration and conflict* (pp. 385–386). Washington, DC: The Urban Institute Press.

Leed, M., & Taylor, J. (2010). *Assessing impact across policy domains: A workshop at the center for strategic and international studies.* Center for Strategic and International Studies. Retrieved February 12, 2011, from http://csis.org/files/publication/110125_assessing_impact_ndap.pdf

Lischer, S. K. (2005). *Dangerous sanctuaries: Refugee camps, civil war, and the dilemmas of humanitarian aid.* Ithaca, NY: Cornell University Press.

Lischer, S. K. (2007). Military intervention and the "force multiplier.". *Global Governance*, *13*, 99–118.

Loyn, D. (2009). *In Afghanistan.* New York: Palgrave Macmillan.

Miakhel, S. (2009). *Understanding Afghanistan: The importance of tribal culture and structure in security and governance.* Pashtoonkhwa. Retrieved July 2, 2011, from http://www.pashtoonkhwa.com/files/books/Miakhel-ImportanceOfTribalStructuresInAfghanistan.pdf

Mosse, D. (2005). *Cultivating development: An ethnography of aid policy and practice.* Ann Arbor, MI: Pluto Press.

Picard, L. A., & Buss, T. F. (2009). *A fragile balance: Re-examining the history of foreign aid, security, and diplomacy.* Sterling, VA: Kumarian Press.

Rasanayagam, A. (2003). *Afghanistan: A modern history*. London: I. B. Tauris and Company, LTD.

Roberts, N. C. (2010). Spanning bleeding boundaries: Humanitarianism, NGOs, and the civilian-military nexus in the post-cold war era. *Public Administration Review, 70*(March), 212–222. doi:10.1111/j.1540-6210.2010.02135_2.x

Slaughter, S. R. (2010). *Expanding the Qawm: Culturally savvy counterinsurgency and nation-building in Afghanistan. Monograph*. Fort Leavenworth, KS: School of Advanced Military Studies, United States Army Command and General Staff College.

Tapper, R. (1983). *The Conflict of Tribe and State in Iran and Afghanistan*. London: Croom Helm.

The Treaty of Versailles. (1919). Retrieved December 27, 2011, from http://history.sandiego.edu/gen/text/versaillestreaty/all440.html

Tuchman, B. W. (1984). *The march of folly*. New York: Alfred A. Knopf, Inc.

Tushman, M., & Romanelli, E. (1985). Organizational evolution: A metamorphosis model of convergence and reorientation. In L. L. Cummings & B. M. Staw (Eds.), *Research in organizational behavior* (Vol. 7, pp. 171–222). Greenwich, CT: JAI Press.

United States Army History Archives. (1947). *The First Year of the Occupation – Occupation Forces in Europe Series 1945-1946*. Retrieved October 2, 2011, from http://www.history.hqusareur.army.mil/Archives/First%20Year/the%20first%20year%202.pdf

United States Central Intelligence Agency. (2012). *The World Factbook*. Retrieved February 9, 2012, from https://www.cia.gov/library/publications/resources/the-world-factbook/

Van de Ven, A. H., & Poole, M. S. (1995). Explaining development and change in organizations. *Academy of Management Review, 20*(3), 510–540. doi:10.2307/258786

Van Meter, R. H. (1979). Herbert Hoover and the economic reconstruction of Europe. In L. E. Gelfand (Ed.), *Herbert Hoover: The great war and its aftermath 1914-23* (pp. 143–181). Iowa City, IA: University of Iowa Press.

Young, D. R. (2006). Complementary, supplementary, or adversarial? Nonprofit-governmental relations. In E. T. Boris & C. E. Steuerle (Eds.), *Nonprofits and government: Collaboration and conflict* (pp. 37–79). Washington, DC: The Urban Institute Press.

KEY TERMS AND DEFINITIONS

Change Capacity: The ability of a society to adapt to stresses and shocks, either endogenous or exogenous, in a cohesive and positive manner.

Counterinsurgency Operations: The use of both military and nonmilitary aspects designed to defeat an insurgency by both providing security for the target population and addressing the root causes of the insurgency.

Jirga: A consensus building forum for making decisions.

Madrassas: The religious schools that produce clerics.

Nation Building: The reconstruction of state infrastructure, to include the physical, political, and social aspects, which have been damaged through conflict.

Pacification: The attempt to create or maintain peace.

Pashtunwali: An almost ubiquitous code of conduct which provides a system of rules and expectations to govern life for Afghans.

Qawm: A social network most closely An über political party, replete with expectations of patronage and the sense of loyalty derived from that patronage.

Chapter 3
Agent–Based Modeling

INTRODUCTION

In 1998 the United Nations General Assembly stated in Resolution 52/167 on page one that they were:

Deeply concerned by the growing number of complex humanitarian emergencies, in particular armed conflicts and post-conflict situations, in the last few years, which have dramatically increased the loss of human lives, suffering of victims, flows of refugees and internally displaced persons, as well as material destruction, which disrupt the development efforts of countries affected, in particular those of developing countries.

Additionally in 1992, via resolution 46/182 the United Nations General Assembly adopted a series of Guiding Principles to strengthen the coordination of international humanitarian emergency assistance. Those principles state in part that:

The magnitude and duration of many emergencies may be beyond the response capacity of many affected countries. International cooperation to address emergency situations and to strengthen the response capacity of affected countries is thus of great importance. Such cooperation should be provided in accordance with international law and national laws. Intergovernmental and non-governmental organizations working impartially and with strictly humanitarian motives should continue to make a significant contribution

DOI: 10.4018/978-1-5225-1782-5.ch003

in supplementing national efforts. ... There is a clear relationship between emergency, rehabilitation and development. In order to ensure a smooth transition from relief to rehabilitation and development, emergency assistance should be provided in ways that will be supportive of recovery and long-term development. Thus, emergency measures should be seen as a step towards long-term development. (Annex, page 50)

Complex adaptive systems are different in that each of their parts follows an individualized set of rules that can vary as they interact within the larger system. There is no overarching set of rules governing the outcome – complex adaptive systems are non-deterministic. The non-deterministic, or stochastic, non-linear behavior of these complex adaptive systems can be extremely difficult to predict. Small variations in initial conditions can cause dramatic changes in outcomes. These variations become problematic to predict because their outcomes vary as the *product* of the system variables versus the *sum* of those variables. The problem as Holland (1995) describes it is that "It is much easier to use mathematics when systems have linear properties that we often expend considerable effort to justify an assumption of linearity" (p.15). Linear models have great difficulties predicting emergent behaviors. The difficulty is so great that the term "black swan" came into vogue thanks to Taleb's (2007) bestselling book, *The black swan: The impact of the highly improbable*. It is precisely these types of events – 9/11, the 2008 financial crisis, the success of the iPod – that causes dramatic change; what Gersick (1991) describes as punctuated equilibrium. These types of events dramatically alter the systems in which they occur and they do not always change them for the better. None of the linear models would have predicted such events because they were caused by outlier variables. The point of agent based modeling and other similar tools for modeling non-linear behavior is to conduct thought experiments to gain insight into the possible; regardless of its probability.

BACKGROUND

Characteristics of Agent Based Modeling

As previously stated, agent based modeling is one of the tools available to researchers studying complex adaptive systems. One of the key differentiating factors of agent based modeling is that the model simulations are constructed from the bottom up versus the top down. Top down models are typically the linear type that use deductive logic that start from a general theory and then develop hypotheses for testing to determine the model's validity in specific instances. Inductive methods can also be utilized to build a theory that starts with specific observations and compiles them into a generalized theory. The trouble is that when these approaches are utilized to describe complex adaptive systems, there are problems with the fit of the model. Additionally, these types of models do not account for emergent behavior which is a hallmark of complex adaptive systems.

Agent based modeling differs from the linear based approach because it is non-deterministic. That means instead of having an end-state of affairs in mind when beginning to design the model, a few critical variables are identified and their key characteristics and relationships are described. This entails identifying the agents (actors) and their behavioral characteristics to include the characteristics of their interactions with each other and the environment. The response characteristics of the environmental variables to each of the agents is also captured and represented within the model. The simulation model algorithm is then allowed to run and the outcome of the simulation can be observed real-time. These simulation runs can be carefully controlled by altering the variables through an interface within the software to create alternative relationships within the simulation. The most important concept within the agent based modeling methodology is that these thought experiments are non-deterministic and optimized to produce emergent behavior through an experimental methodology.

One of the early models used to describe non-linear behavior in systems was the famous Lotka-Volterra model (Holland, 1995). The equations for the model were first described by Alfred Lotka (1920) to represent undamped chemical reactions and then further refined by Vito Volterra (1926) to apply to predator-prey interactions (Evans & Findley, 1999). The equations are first-order ordinary differential equations. Suppose that N(t) is the number of prey at time t, and P(t) is the predator population. Then the two equations that describe the system are $\frac{dN}{dt} = N(a - bP)$ and $\frac{dP}{dt} = P(cN - d)$ where (a) is the birth rate of prey; (-b) is the reduction in the number of prey due to predation; (c) is the reproduction rate of predators as a result of consuming prey; and (d) is the natural death rate of the predators. The graphs of the resultant solutions to these equations show an oscillation around a stationary point with the graph representing the prey population always leading the predator population. In Figure 1, the number of predators and prey will eventually reach a dynamic equilibrium at some point within this set of elliptical solutions. The system does not have to begin within one of these solution sets but it will eventually settle within one. The analysis of this system is not overly complex and it demonstrates the zero equilibrium solution which is unstable, as well as a positive equilibrium, which is neutrally stable, thereby providing periodic solutions within the bounds of this equilibrium. Unfortunately this model contains obvious limitations; primarily that in the absence of predators, the prey population grows unbounded. This basic model however has proven to be useful in many fields and become a classic in non-linear systems such as population biology,

chemical kinetics, and parasite-host epidemiology. Additional refinements and improvements have been proposed, making the Lotka-Volterra model one of the most studied systems in mathematical biology (Evans & Findley 1999).

A very simplistic example of the utility of agent based modeling is Holland's predator / prey system described earlier utilizing the Lotka-Volterra model. Instead of solving a series of differential equations, a researcher can access an agent based modeling software library and select an appropriate

Figure 1. Predator-prey dynamic equilibrium

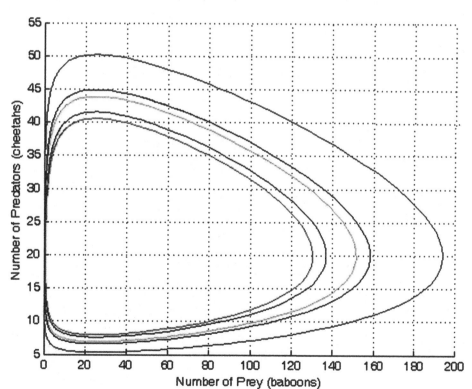

simulation such as the "Wolf Sheep Predation" model built by Wilensky (1997) in NetLogo. The simulation involves two agents, wolves and sheep, moving randomly through a simulated landscape environment in which the grass re-grows at a scalable rate. The other attributes that can be varied are the initial number of each agent type, the rate of reproduction of the agents and the amount of sustenance each agent gains from eating. The simulation has a non-deterministic quality because of the random number generator embedded in the NetLogo code that influences the placement of the agents on the landscape and relative to each other as well as their initial energy state and their propensity to breed. This stochastic quality is also present in the code used for the simulation in this research. Figure 2 is a screen shot of the simulation interface at time zero. As the simulation runs, the sheep consume grass which re-grows at a fixed rate, the sheep reproduce at the set rate, the wolves prey on the sheep, and the wolves reproduce at a fixed rate. The point to notice within the simulation is the relative populations show similar oscillations as predicted by the Lotka-Volterra equations (see circled interface graph in Figure 3). This simulation can then generate a series of experiments by changing the parameters of the simulation such as the reproduction rates of either the predators, prey or both. It can also examine the outcomes of

Figure 2. Simulation interface at time zero

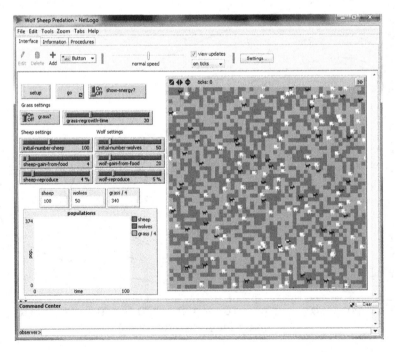

Figure 3. Interface graph

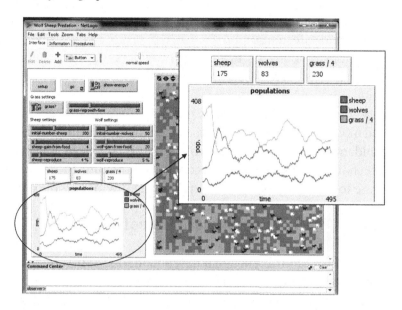

environmental changes such as the rate of growth of the grass. All of these factors can have an outcome on the populations of each agent type as well as the environment. This illustrates one of the primary attributes of agent based modeling: the variables can be isolated to provide experimental data sets in ways that are not possible with other methods or in the 'real world.'

The Use of Agent Based Modeling in Various Research Fields

A look through the calls for papers in various symposiums being held around the world helps to demonstrate the breadth and reach of complexity science and the versatility of agent based modeling as a useful tool in those studies. In a call for papers for a conference called "Human Complexity 2012, The First Annual Conference on Complexity and Human Experience, Modeling Complexity in the Humanities and Social Sciences" to be held at the Center for Advanced Research in the Humanities at the University of North Carolina, Charlotte, the list of topics was particularly broad based:

- The propagation of beliefs, ideas and ideologies
- The effect of individual action on global economies
- Social structure among pre-historic peoples

- Discovery of early trends and indicators of social and economic change
- The relationship between organizational/societal structure and the flow of energy and information
- The relationship between healthcare providers, patients, Internet, and social media (http://www.complexity.uncc.edu)

In addition to the topics, there have been similar conferences to discuss agent based modeling advances in defense technology and tactics, home land security, epidemiology, as well as areas of the natural sciences. As agent based modeling techniques and software tools continue to mature, the fields of study will continue to expand and add to the understanding of complex systems.

Agent Based Modeling Software Selection

There is a robust list of different agent based modeling software platforms to choose from. Appendix (A) contains the inclusive list of fifty-four software platforms that were initially considered. Each of these platforms has attributes that make it popular in the diverse universe of fields that utilize agent based models to conduct experiments. Many platforms also contain attributes that made them inappropriate for either the researcher or the characteristics of this particular study. This list was reduced to a final four to review for consideration: NetLogo, MASON, Repast, and Swarm. The primary considerations for selection revolved around finding a platform that was compatible with a limited degree of programming experience, compatibility with a Windows operating system, and a free or low cost license agreement. Those attributes are summarized in Table 1.

From this list of finalists, NetLogo was the software package selected. While all of the software packages have reasonably good documentation, NetLogo's heritage as an educational software package made it superior for use by neophyte programmers. Additionally, it contains an effort checking function that enables rapid trouble shooting of the program. These were the primary considerations for this research effort. Other, more functionally complex modeling scenarios may find Swarm (which came in a close second in this selection process) to be a superior simulation platform. NetLogo does not require the same level of organizational programming discipline that the other programs do because it requires all of the code to reside in one file; there are not multiple program files to track and organize such as the layout of the environment, the attributes of the agents, the movements of the agents, etcetera (Railsback, Lytinen, and Jackson 2006). Otherwise, the execution

Table 1. Comparison of ABM software

Platform	Primary Domain	License	Program Language	Operating System	User Support
MASON	General purpose;	Academic Free License (open source)	Java	Any Java Platform (1.3 or higher)	Mailing list; documentation; Tutorials; third party extensions; reference papers; API
NetLogo	Social & natural sciences; Help beginning users get started authoring models	Free, not open source	NetLogo	Any Java Virtual Machine, version 5 or later.	Documentation; FAQ; selected references; tutorials; third party extensions; defect list; mailing lists
Repast	Social sciences	BSD - Berkley Software Distribution	Java	Java version 1.4, Windows (Repast.net)	Documentation; mailing list; defect list; reference papers; external tools; tutorials; FAQ; examples
Swarm	General purpose agent based	Free, Cougaar Open Source License (COSL)	Java; Objective-C	Windows; Mac OS X	Wiki; tutorials; examples; documentation; FAQ; selected publications; mailing lists

Adapted from Nikolai & Madey 2009

speed of NetLogo was in the midrange of the final software packages reviewed and the ease of use and extensive model library made the final choice straight-forward.

DESCRIPTION OF THE MODEL USED FOR THIS STUDY

The model used in the experimental portion of this study is a derivative of the NetLogo Wolf Sheep Predation model (Wilensky, 1997). Table 3.2 illustrates the basic interface and provides a guide through the discussion of the model's construction. The selection and setting of the variables used during the experiments is discussed in detail in the following chapter.

Table 3. Agent energy changes

Agent	Action	Outcome
Insurgent	Moves across light patch Moves across dark patch	No Change Gains energy
International & NGO agent	Moves across light patch Moves across dark patch	Gains energy Losses energy
Incumbent Government agent	Moves across light patch Moves across dark patch	Gains energy No change

Landscape

The landscape of this model includes the following variables and setting parameters. Variable one (see Table 2) is the "level of violence" that is present in the simulation. This interface determines the amount of energy (or life force units) that each agent sacrifices to attack another. In a highly contested environment, there is a cost for one group to attack another. Western military forces may have an advantage in terms of pure fire power and destructive force but the insurgents have the advantage of local terrain knowledge. When all sides are prepared for attack, each will extract a toll from the other for an attack and this variable sets the level of overall preparedness for all the agents in the simulation.

Table 2. Variables and setting parameters

Variable	Attribute	Range	Units
Level of violence	Energy cost to attack	10 - 100	1
Initial number of insurgents	Beginning number of insurgent combatants	0 - 250	1
Initial number of international combatant & NGO agents	Beginning number of international agent combatants, civilian staff & NGO personnel	0 - 250	1
Initial number of incumbent government agents	Beginning number of incumbent government agent combatants	0 - 250	1
Government legitimacy	Ability to recruit from the population	1 - 20	1
Insurgent legitimacy	Ability to recruit from the population	1 - 20	1
Government gain from indigenous population	Support given to the agents in the form of energy units	0 - 10	0.1
Insurgent gain from indigenous population	Support given to the agents in the form of energy units	0 - 10	0.1
Level of coordination between international governmental & NGO agents	Increased coordination causes individuals within the population to become more sympathetic toward indigenous government	0 - 2.0	0.1

Agent Variables

The agent energy level is defined as the life force an individual agent has. This energy is expended through actions taken to include simple existence (which would be the agent's base metabolism rate). Each agent type has a beginning energy level that must remain above zero or else the individual agent dies. For the international agent types, which include international development agents, nongovernmental organization agents, and military agents, their initial energy level is set at a random number between one and twenty. The governmental agent types have their initial energy set at a random number between one and five times the "government gain from the population" interface control {set energy random (5 * govt-gain-from-pop)}. The insurgent agent type has a similar attribute with the formula for their initial energy level being set between one and five times the "insurgent gain from the population" interface control {set energy random (5 * ins-gain-from-pop)}.

Variables two, three, and four (see Table 2) are simply the number of agents of each type initially present in the landscape. These numbers are meant to be a representative ratio of the agents within the context of the simulation. The agents move about an environment that is represented by "patches" in NetLogo terms. Within this simulation space, there are 2,600 patches that represent the indigenous population. Those patches vary in color with regard to their affiliations or sympathies. White patches are loyal to the incumbent government and the black are loyal to the insurgency. The brown patches are neutral. Initially upon set up, each patch color is randomly assigned and randomly distributed throughout the simulation space with equal numbers of black, brown, and white patches.

The indigenous population (the patches) changes color as they interact with the various agents. Insurgents passing over the dark colored patches gather energy (or life force in the form of moral and material support) from them and cause them to darken at a preset rate. Government and international agents have a similar effect on light colored patches by causing them to lighten while gaining energy. International agents lose energy when they come in contact with a dark colored patch (insurgency sympathizer), but they are the exception. When a patch has reached white or black, its color change stops in that direction but it continues to give energy to those preferred agents that pass over it.

Variables five and six (see Table 2) account for the legitimacy of both the incumbent government and that of the insurgent agent cause, respectively. Legitimacy is a latent variable that is a combination of other more directly accessible and measurable variables. For the government, this roll up of variables includes the relative degree of corruption, the degree of fit with local culture (are changes counter to societal norms being forced), security for the local population, and perceived efforts at good governance (economic development and support of infrastructure, civil law, and providing day to day needs such as potable water). For the insurgent side, the less successful the incumbent government is at governance, the greater the appeal of an alternative cause. The insurgency gains legitimacy by controlling unincorporated areas of the country where the government has little or no control. By establishing a shadow government and operating with lower levels of corruption and more effective governance, greater levels of legitimacy are established (Kilcullen, 2010). This can be seen in this scenario as establishing pockets of theocratic rule (Sharia Law). This state of affairs however, can be a double edged sword for the insurgent. A repressive and oppressive rule can have a counterproductive effect on the attitudes of the ruled population.

There is a paradox that can occur when good governance is pursued by the incumbent government without regard for the change capacity of the society. Variable five is the simulation variable used to account for that situation within this simulation. The end result of the influence in this simulation is the effect on recruitment for both types of agents. This effect is very similar (in fact the coding is the same) to that of reproduction in the Wolf Sheep Predation model (Wilensky, 1997). The greater the legitimacy for either agent set, the greater the likelihood of increased numbers through recruitment from the general population.

Variables seven and eight (see Table 2) are the amount of support the competing agents receive from the patches. This correlates to and should move in conjunction with the legitimacy variable for each agent type. This attribute is separated in this model as a programming convenience because the support variable provides sustenance to the existing agents while the legitimacy variable provides for new agents. There may be circumstances that would cause these two variables to move counter to each other. For Example, a radical school corrupting the young to join an insurgent movement that the general population finds abhorrent is not a case type that is investigated in this research. Each movement by an agent causes the agent to expend energy. The only way an agent can gain energy is by contacting (moving across) a patch representing a population segment (see Table 3)

Finally, variable nine (see Table 2) is the level of coordination of activities between the international governmental agents, the military arm of the international government agents, and the nongovernmental agents, within the scope of the operation attempting to bring stability to the society. In this study, the act of bringing stability is more specifically defined as: "… maintain or reestablish a safe and secure environment, provide essential governmental services, emergency infrastructure reconstruction, and humanitarian relief" (Joint Publication 3-07, 2008, p. vi). The level of cooperation variable is operationalized in this model as an attribute of how much of a color change a patch will undergo when contacting international type agents. If the level of coordination among the international agencies is zero, the color change for the patch is zero. As the level of coordination becomes greater, the degree of positive color change for the patch increases. The opposite occurs when the international agencies are acting in a less coordinated (domain conflicted) manner. When domain conflicted partners attempt to provide stability, they frequently achieve suboptimal or even counterproductive outcomes (Roberts, 2010; Lischer, 2007). Controlling this variable in relation to the other variables in the simulation allows for an examination of the relative importance of each of the variables in the final outcome.

The status of these variables is controlled through the interface with graphic type controls that allow the user to adjust the value by activation of the mouse. The resulting outcomes are tracked both graphically in the simulation space as well as through a series of pen plots and counters which show the relative success of each of the agent types as well as the degree of stability being brought to the simulation through the surrogate of the "loyalist" patches. The logic of this model is represented in figure 3.4. The relatively plain language of NetLogo instructions make them relatively intuitive to follow. The specifics of why each of the variables is set to a specific parameter will be covered in detail in the next chapter.

RESEARCH QUESTION

The understanding and integration of military force with nongovernmental organizations in the area of operations are critical to reestablishing stability within a fractured society. Will the United Nations' agencies be met with a handshake or a fist by the populations they are attempting to help? Understanding the military / nongovernmental organization interaction is a crucial item of the policy framework that determines feasible courses of action to international governmental agencies. Further, what level and type of integration should be attempted? At present, United Nations agencies have no clear structures or formal processes for determining how to either integrate the efforts of nongovernmental organizations (other than ad hoc) with coincident military interests or neutralize nongovernmental organizations with counter interests.

Figure 4.

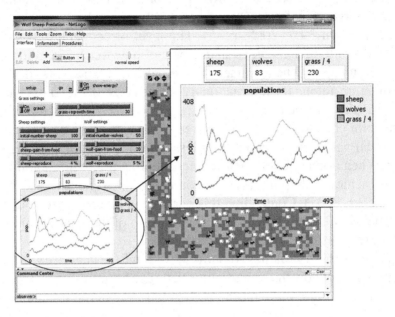

This lack of structure is thought to reduce the effectiveness of stability and development efforts both in terms of direct and indirect mission success. Additionally, these issues exhibit non-linear behavior. Unexpected events – such as a coup or assassination - may change the course of history. It seems that small differences in inputs can become enormous differences in output.

This phenomenon is referred to by James Gleick (1988, p. 8) as a "sensitive dependence on initial conditions." These are the type of problems that defy explanation by traditional top-down theories of social reality. This research tests the theory that a high level of coordination between military and nongovernmental organization operations can be a force multiplier in the effort to bring stability to a strife torn region. The concept of utilizing a force multiplier when put forward by military planners is the use of a technique or tactic that has the effect of reducing the number of personnel or equipment needed to accomplish a desired task. It is an attempt to achieve a step wise jump in efficiency. The primary research question is: "Does a high level of coordination between military and nongovernmental organization activities have a force multiplying effect?" Further conditions examined are: "Does the level of violence present in the area of operations or the levels of legitimacy for both the indigenous government and the insurgency movement, have an impact on the levels of effectiveness – if any – derived from this military / nongovernmental organization coordination?" Finally, "Does a 'surge' or rapid change in the number of international agents, primarily military, provide an outsized impact on the outcomes of the counterinsurgency efforts?"

The outcomes of the simulations of this model are straightforward. In each run, either the incumbent government or the insurgency dominates. If the incumbent government dominates a particular simulation run, that outcome is a surrogate for stability having been achieved and the policy combination utilized by the international governmental agencies being successful. The opposite is true if the insurgent agents dominate. For each set of combinations for setting the policy variables, thirty simulations runs are performed and recorded. The crucial concept to keep in mind with agent based modeling simulations however is that they are not an end to themselves. These simulations are designed to generate data from the interaction of the agents within an environment that controls for exogenous variables. This is not to say that emergent behavior will not be observed; it frequently is. The goal is to generate a data set of outcomes that enables statistical hypotheses testing to be conducted regarding the influence of the variables. The specifics of the statistical methodology are covered in the next chapter.

REFERENCES

DeCoster, J. (1998). *Overview of Factor Analysis* (Class notes). Retrieved October 22, 2011, from http://www.stat-help.com/notes.html

Evans, C. M., & Findley, G. L. (1999). Analytic solutions to a family of Lotka-Volterra related differential equations. *Journal of Mathematical Chemistry*, 25(2/3), 181–189. doi:10.1023/A:1019184417025

Gersick, C. J. (1991). Revolutionary change theories: A multilevel exploration of the punctuated equilibrium paradigm. *Academy of Management Review*, 16(1), 10–36. doi:10.5465/AMR.1991.4278988

Gleick, J. (1988). *Chaos: The making of a new science*. New York: Penguin Books.

Holland, J. H. (1995). *Hidden order: How adaptation builds complexity*. Reading, MA: Helix Books.

Hox, J. J., & Bechger, T. M. (1998). An introduction to structural equation modeling. *Family Science Review*, 11, 354–373.

Human Complexity 2012, The First Annual Conference on Complexity and Human Experience, Modeling Complexity in the Humanities and Social Sciences to be held at the Center for Advanced Research in the Humanities at the University of North Carolina, Charlotte (Call for papers). (n.d.). Retrieved February 11, 2012, from http://www.complexity.uncc.edu

Joint Publication 3-07. (2008). Retrieved February 4, 2011, from http://www.dtic.mil/doctrine/new_pubs/jp3_07.pdf

Kenny, D. A., & Judd, C. M. (1984). Estimating the nonlinear and interactive effects of latent variables. *Psychological Bulletin, 96*(I), 201–210. doi:10.1037/0033-2909.96.1.201

Kilcullen, D. (2010). *Counterinsurgency redux*. Retrieved December 27, 2011, from http://smallwarsjournal.com/documents/kilcullen1.pdf

Lischer, S. K. (2007). Military intervention and the "force multiplier.". *Global Governance, 13*, 99–118.

Nikolai, C., & Madey, G. (2009). Tools of the Trade: A survey of various agent based modeling platforms. *Journal of Artificial Societies and Social Simulation, 12*(2), 2. Retrieved from http://jasss.soc.surrey.ac.uk/12/2/2.html

Railsback, S. F., Lytinen, S. F., & Jackson, S. K. (2006). Agent-based simulation platforms: Review and development recommendations. *Simulations, 82*(9), 609–623. doi:10.1177/0037549706073695

Roberts, N. C. (2010). Spanning bleeding boundaries: Humanitarianism, NGOs, and the civilian-military nexus in the post-cold war era. *Public Administration Review, 70*(March), 212–222. doi:10.1111/j.1540-6210.2010.02135_2.x

Taleb, N. N. (2007). *The black swan: The impact of the highly improbable*. New York: Random House Publishing Group.

United Nations General Assembly Resolution 46/182. (1992). *Strengthening of the coordination of humanitarian emergency assistance of the United Nations: Guiding principles*. New York: United Nations.

United Nations General Assembly Resolution 52/167. (1998). *Safety and security of humanitarian personnel*. New York: United Nations.

Wilensky, U. (1999). *NetLogo*. Center for Connected Learning and Computer-Based Modeling, Northwestern University. Retrieved February 4, 2011, from http://ccl.northwestern.edu/netlogo/

Zimmerman, B., Lindberg, C., & Plsek, P. (1998). *A complexity science primer: what is complexity science and why should I learn about it?*. Irving, TX: VHA Publishing.

Zyphur, M. J., Barsky, A. P., & Zhang, Z. (2012). Advances in leadership research. In D. V. Day & J. Antonakis (Eds.), *The theory and nature of leadership* (pp. 66–95). Thousand Oaks, CA: Sage Publications, Inc.

KEY TERMS AND DEFINITIONS

Complex Adaptive Systems (CAS): Dynamic, interacting networks of individuals that generate collective behavior that mutates to adapt to changing conditions.

Emergence: The formation of larger systems or patterns that develop through the interactions among smaller or simpler entities that do not resemble the properties of the larger systems they form.

Factor Analysis: A statistical tool in which observed data are expressed as functions of a number of possible causes in order to find which are the most important.

Linear Structural Relations (LISREL): A statistical modeling technique that combines factor analyses with the simultaneous estimation of structural relationships between a set of extracted latent factors.

Lotka-Volterra Model: A mathematical model of the competitive interactions of species pursuing some limiting resource.

Non-Deterministic: Stochastic or random.

Non-Linear Behavior: The outputs of a system is not proportional to the inputs which causes the behavior of the system to appear chaotic and unpredictable.

Chapter 4
The Simulation Presented in the ODD Protocol

INTRODUCTION

It seems that small differences in inputs can become enormous differences in output. This phenomenon is referred to by James Gleick (1988, p. 8) as a "sensitive dependence on initial conditions." These are problems that defy explanation by traditional top-down theories of social reality because the top-down theories tend to operate in a linear paradigm. The difficulty in utilizing statistical tools, even those as advanced as structural equation modeling, which subsumes path analysis, OLS regression, ANOVA, and others is that it is extremely difficult to test the interaction among latent variables. The results from agent based models allow for addressing system aspects that these other models have not; such as transient, nonequilibrium conditions and dependence on initial conditions, which is the intent of this study (North & Macal, 2007).

THE ODD PROTOCOL

Verification testing of this model was conducted by observing the outputs of the model at the extremes of the simulation to ensure that the results moved in predicted directions. Validation of the model involved comparisons of the model outcomes to a series of case studies involving counterinsurgency operations and the delivery of development aid. The case studies utilized included:

DOI: 10.4018/978-1-5225-1782-5.ch004

- Police in the lead with military support or vice versa (Sepp, 2004).
- The timing of development aid delivery vis-à-vis the stage of the counterinsurgency campaign – either early or late (Barlow, 2010).
- The integration of local population into security forces – either high or low (Barton, 2010; Megahan, 2010; Sepp, 2004).
- The level of local population inclusion in development aid delivery – either high or low (Brinkerhoff, 2010; Guttieri, 2010; Pimbo, 2010).
- The level of local institutional development - either high or low (Brinkerhoff 2010; Pandya, 2010; Sepp, 2004; von Hippel, 2010).
- The level of security from violence - either high or low (Guttieri, 2010; Sepp, 2004).
- The level of local population cooperation with counterinsurgency forces vis-à-vis the insurgents - either high or low (Galula, 1964).
- The level of coordination with government agencies – either high or low (Curry, 2010; Szayna, et al., 2009).
- The propensity to operate independently from other organizations either NGO or governmental - either high or low (Curry 2010).
- The religious affiliation of the NGO – either affiliated with the local religious majority, minority, or secular (de Haan, 2009; Flanigan, 2010).

The case studies also informed the initial settings and ranges of the model variables in the simulation.

Purpose

This study tests two hypotheses. First, that a high level of coordination between military and NGO operations, and the subsequent positive affect engendered in the population, can be a force multiplier in the effort to bring stability to a strife torn region. The second hypothesis being that a "surge" of Western personnel, either military or a combination of military and support personnel, will have a positive impact on security and therefore increase the positive affect engendered in the population by the Western intervention. The research question is: "Does the positive affect generated by a high level of coordination between military and NGO activities have a force multiplying (nonlinear) effect?" and "What is the impact of a surge in the numbers of international forces in the region?" Further conditions examined are: "Does the level of violence present in the area of operations, or the levels of legitimacy of the indigenous government have an impact on the levels of effectiveness – if any – derived from this military-NGO coordination?"

Entities, State Variables, and Scales

The landscape of this model includes the following variables and setting parameters. The landscape the mobile agent types traverse is a square grid of 51 X 51 patches. The length of one time step is 3 months: 4 time steps equal one year. Table 1 contains the remaining variables and scales.

Process Overview and Scheduling

There are several processes that occur within each time step of this model. Each mobile agent is asked to move (which uses energy); to attack an opposing agent if contacted (again expending energy); and to die if energy reserves are depleted. Two agent types, insurgent agents and incumbent government agents, reproduce during each tick. The patches (which are stationary agents) interact with each of the mobile agents. Each of the patches changes color to represent their loyalties to the respective mobile agents. As the mobile agents traverse a patch, they have an influence on the color (loyalty) of the

Table 1. Variables and setting parameters

Variable	Attribute	Range	Settings
Level of violence	Energy cost to attack	10 - 100	40, 95
Initial number of insurgents	Beginning number of insurgent combatants	0 - 250	30
Initial number of international combatant & NGO agents	Beginning number of international agent combatants & civilian staff	0 - 250	20
Secondary number of international combatant & NGO agents	Beginning number of international agent combatants & NGO staff if no surge	0 - 250	10
Initial number of incumbent government agents	Beginning number of incumbent government agent combatants	0 - 250	30
Government legitimacy	Ability to recruit from the population	1 - 20	3.5, 3.92
Insurgent legitimacy	Ability to recruit from the population	1 - 20	4.0
Government gain from indigenous population	Support given to the agents in the form of energy units	0 - 10	3.0
Insurgent gain from indigenous population	Support given to the agents in the form of energy units	0 - 10	3.0
International gain from indigenous population	Support given to the agents in the form of energy units	0 – 10	2.0
Level of coordination between international governmental & NGO agents	Increased coordination causes individuals within the population to become more sympathetic toward indigenous government	0 - 2.0	0.0, 2.0

patch. Patches loyal to a mobile agent provide that agent with energy thereby assisting the mobile agent's cause. The patch's color can change over time based upon the varying amount of contact it has with various mobile agents.

DESIGN CONCEPTS

Basic Principles

The basic principle addressed by this model is the attempt by the mobile agents, representing the combatants, to win favor of the stationary agents, the population. This concept is addressed by setting up feedback loops between the mobile and stationary agents; as the mobile agents have success influencing the stationary agents, the stationary agents in turn provide support to those same mobile agent types. This adaptive behavior reflects the simple empirical rule that control (or at least acquiescence) of the population is necessary to prevail in counterinsurgency warfare which is therefore the objective of the mobile agents (Galula, 1964). The model itself is based upon a predator / prey interaction with a twist: each subtype of the mobile agents acts as both predator and prey in their interactions with other mobile agent subtypes. In other words they fight each other when they interact. The violence of the interaction is an adjustable variable in the model. The more successful an agent subtype is in survival and replication both enabled by utilizing energy gained through contact with "friendly" segments of the population, the more successful that subtype will be in driving out the opposing subtype.

Learning, Prediction

In this model, the behavior of the agents is held constant so the agents are not given the capacity to 'learn' and alter their behavior. There are several reasons for doing so. First, the main purpose of the model is to simulate the response from the indigenous population to differing strategies used with regard to the mobile agents – the international combatants and NGO staff, and the insurgent combatants and their sympathizers. Second, one of the assumptions used in building the model is that the near term behavior of the agents is fixed until the outcomes of their behavior become apparent. For the span of time involved in the counterinsurgency scenario, the agent behaviors tend to be ridged with learning taking place upon reflection when hostilities have ended. This limitation was apparent in the after action reports and case studies reviewed during the model design. Finally, to include learning in the model, a much higher level of agent complexity would be involved due to the mitigating influences of the deep structures of the society, which were not the target of this investigation, so there is no 'prediction' element built into this model. The sensing, interaction and stochastic processes used in the model are described in the following narrative, which includes a discussion of the variable settings, initialization, and sub-models used.

Sensing, Interaction, and Stochastic Processes

Variable one (see table 4.1) is the "level of violence" that is present in the simulation. This interface determines the amount of energy (or life force units) that each agent sacrifices to attack another. In a highly contested environment, there is a cost for one group to attack another. Western military forces may have an advantage in terms of pure fire power and destructive force but the insurgents have the advantage of local terrain knowledge. When all sides are prepared for attack, each will extract a toll from the other for an attack and this variable sets the level of overall preparedness for all the agents in the simulation.

The agent energy level is defined as the life force an individual agent has. Another metaphor for the energy level used in the model is the will to preserver in the mission. The energy levels for agents are set relative to each other based upon agent type. This energy is expended through actions taken to include simple existence (which would be the agent's base metabolism rate). Each agent type has a beginning energy level that must remain above zero or else the individual agent dies. The energy level for each agent type has a stochastic element because individual agents within each type are heterogeneous in their motivations and abilities to reflect the reality of the populations they are modeling. For the international agent types, which include international development agents, nongovernmental organization agents, and military agents, their initial energy level is set at a random number between one and twenty. This level was chosen because it is within the range of the other agent types but it is not influenced by the indigenous population but rather by the myriad of influences ranging from donor motives to home nation public support. The governmental agent types have their initial energy set at a random number between one and five times the "government gain from the population" interface control. The insurgent agent type has a similar attribute with the formula for their initial energy level being set between one and five times the "insurgent gain from the population" interface control. All of the agents are moving at random within the simulation.

Variables two, three, and four (see table 1) are simply the number of stationary agents (patches) of each type initially present in the landscape. Within this simulation space, there are 2,601 patches that represent the indigenous population. Those patches vary in color with regard to their affiliations or sympathies. White patches are loyal to the incumbent government and the black are loyal to the insurgency. The brown patches are neutral. Initially upon set up, each patch color is randomly assigned and randomly distributed throughout the simulation space with equal numbers of black, brown, and white patches.

DETAILS

Initialization, Input Data, Sub-Models

The indigenous population (the patches) change color as they interact with the various agents. Insurgents passing over the dark colored patches gather energy (or life force in the form of moral and material support) from them and cause them to darken at a preset rate. Government and international agents have a similar effect on light colored patches by causing them to lighten while gaining energy. International agents lose energy when they come in contact with a dark colored patch (insurgency sympathizer), but they are the exception. When a patch has reached white or black, its color change stops in that direction but it continues to give energy to those preferred agents that pass over it.

Variables five and six (see table 4.1) account for the legitimacy of both the incumbent government and that of the insurgent agent cause, respectively. Legitimacy is a latent variable that is a combination of other more directly accessible and measurable variables. For the government, this roll up of variables includes the relative degree of corruption, the degree of fit with local culture (are changes counter to societal norms being forced), security for the local population, and perceived efforts at good governance (economic development and support of infrastructure, civil law, and providing day to day needs such as potable water). For the insurgent side, the less successful the incumbent government is at governance, the greater the appeal of an alternative cause. The insurgency gains legitimacy by controlling unincorporated areas of the country where the government has little or no control. By establishing a shadow government and operating with lower levels of corruption and more effective governance, greater levels of legitimacy are established (Kilcullen, 2010). This can be seen in this scenario as establishing pockets of theocratic rule (Sharia Law). This state of affairs however, can be a double edged sword for the insurgent. A repressive and oppressive rule can have a counterproductive effect on the attitudes of the ruled population.

Variables seven and eight (see table 4.1) are the amount of support the competing agents receive from the patches. This correlates to and should move in conjunction with the legitimacy variable for each agent type. This attribute is separated in this model as a programming convenience because the support variable provides sustenance to the existing agents while the legitimacy variable provides for new agents. There may be circumstances that would cause these two variables to move counter to each other. For example, a radical school corrupting the young to join an insurgent movement, that the general population finds abhorrent, is not a case type that is investigated in this research. Each movement by an agent causes the agent to expend energy. The only way an agent can gain energy is by contacting (moving across) a patch representing a population segment (see Table 2).

Finally, variable nine (see Table 1) is the level of coordination of activities between the international governmental agents, the military arm of the international government agents, and the nongovernmental agents, within the scope of the operation attempting to bring stability to the society. In this study, the act of bringing stability is more specifically defined as: "… maintain or reestablish a safe and secure environment, provide essential governmental services, emergency infrastructure reconstruction, and humanitarian relief" (Joint Publication 3-07, 2008, p. vi). The level of cooperation variable is operationalized in this model as an attribute of how much of a color change a patch will undergo when contacting international type agents. If the level of coordination among the international agencies is zero, the color change for the patch is zero. As the level of coordination becomes greater, the degree of positive color change for the patch increases. The opposite occurs when the international agencies are acting in a less coordinated (domain conflicted) manner. When domain conflicted partners attempt to provide stabil-

Table 2. Agent energy changes

Agent	Action	Outcome
Insurgent	Moves across light patch Moves across dark patch	No Change Gains energy
International & NGO agent	Moves across light patch Moves across dark patch	Gains energy Loses energy
Incumbent Government agent	Moves across light patch Moves across dark patch	Gains energy No change

ity, they frequently achieve suboptimal or even counterproductive outcomes (Roberts, 2010; Lischer, 2007). Controlling this variable in relation to the other variables in the simulation allows for an examination of the relative importance of each of the variables in the final outcome.

There were 16,000 simulation runs conducted varying the primary research variables against the secondary research variables (see Table 3). There were three variables adjusted within the simulation runs; the level of cooperation between international agents, the level of violence within the simulation scenario, and the level of legitimacy of the incumbent government. When each of these variables was adjusted, the others were held constant yielding the matrix shown in Table 3. In this type of scenario, agent based modeling allows for the isolation of variables in a dynamic environment.

Earlier in this discussion, we considered the nine variables that are adjustable within the framework of this agent based model. There are four variables that remain static during all of the simulation runs. These variables were the initial number of insurgent agents, the initial number of incumbent government agents, and the initial number of international agents (these agent numbers were reduced by fifty percent in the last four simulation run sets), and are shown in Table 1. The ratio represented in the model of thirty, twenty, and thirty respectively is an equal number of government and insurgent agents (thirty) versus twenty international agents. There were multiple reasons for the selection of this ratio. According to the Brookings Afghanistan Index (Livingston & O'Hanlon, 2011) there were just over 200,000

Table 3. Simulation execution matrix

Initial runs	Level of coordination low	Level of coordination medium	Level of coordination high
Level of violence low / Level of legitimacy low	1000 Runs	1000 Runs	1000 Runs
Level of violence low / Level of legitimacy high	1000 Runs	1000 Runs	1000 Runs
Level of violence high / Level of legitimacy low	1000 Runs	1000 Runs	1000 Runs
Level of violence high / Level of legitimacy high	1000 Runs	1000 Runs	1000 Runs
Secondary runs	Level of coordination low		Level of coordination high
Level of violence low / Level of legitimacy low	1000 Runs		
Level of violence low / Level of legitimacy high			1000 Runs
Level of violence high / Level of legitimacy low	1000 Runs		
Level of violence high / Level of legitimacy high			1000 Runs

international agents in Afghanistan at the end of 2011. Of those, roughly 120,000 are combat troops and the remainders are civilian contractors, non-military governmental employees, and nongovernmental organizational personnel. The Afghan government is fielding a security force of just over 300,000 including both the Afghan National Army and the Afghan National Police force. The insurgency in Afghanistan is a bit more difficult to pin down. According to the same Brookings document, there is a core of 30,000 insurgents operating at any giving time within Afghanistan. With these types of force ratios, the insurgency should have been stopped with relative ease; but instead, insurgent attacks have increased fourfold and security of the population is hardly guaranteed (Livingston & O'Hanlon 2011).

The question becomes, how does a small cadre of determined insurgents have an effect as though they have ten times that number? One of the dominant factors within this scenario is that as late as November of 2010, up to ten percent of the Afghan people had a favorable view of the Taliban and nine percent would rather have the Taliban ruling the country (ABC News/ BBC/ARD Poll, "Afghanistan: Where Things Stand", released December 6, 2010). In a country of almost thirty-three million, having over three million desiring to have the primary component of the insurgency regain control of the country is significant. The other critical issue is the size of the illicit economy within Afghanistan. The opium trade approaches $1.6 billion with the legitimate economic GDP standing at $17 billion (United Nations Office on Drugs and Crime, 2011). The opium trade is almost twenty percent greater than the general revenue intake of the Afghan government (Livingston & O'Hanlon, 2011).

Researchers at the World Bank argued that areas of Afghanistan became a fragmented narco-state in which local drug lords took control of district- and provincial-level state institutions of government with the assistance of insurgent groups. Compounding these issues are the relative differences in pay scales for insurgent fighters versus those employed by the Afghan government. (Jones, 2008, p. 48). The average daily pay for Afghan soldiers and police is under three dollars while the insurgents are paid between five and ten dollars per day (Ackerman, 2009; O'Hanlon & Livingston, 2011; Livingston & O'Hanlon, 2011). Additionally, the recruiting ground for insurgent fighters is rich with over 352,000 internally displaced persons, most of whom live below the poverty line (forty-two percent of the total Afghan population lives below the poverty line) of fourteen dollars per month of income (Livingston & O'Hanlon 2011).

Given the level of poverty, the corrupting influence of a robust opium trade, and significant insurgent sympathies across the population, a multiplier of ten is a conservative estimate for the relative force fielded by the insurgent groups. This puts the number of insurgents operating in the simulation at an equivalent strength to that of the government. It is important to note that during the runs of this simulation, both the insurgent agent population numbers as well as the incumbent government agent population numbers can increase in keeping with the concept of each side recruiting from within the indigenous population. The international agents cannot increase their numbers as the simulation moves forward in time. This stipulation is in place to keep the perspective of the unstable state maintaining sovereignty during the course of the simulation.

The other ratios that remain fixed for all of the simulation runs are the government and insurgent energy gains from contact with the population (see table 1). These variables (insurgent gains from the population and government gains from the population) are set at three (3) which is a relative setting, not an absolute indication of a physical transfer of energy as discussed in the preceding chapter. Once again, this measure is a latent variable that is a combination of several factors such as respect within society, the feeling on the part of the belligerents that they are making a positive impact on the everyday lives of their fellow citizens, and the reflection of the citizenry's view of the role the groups are playing within the greater context of society. These attributes are difficult to quantify in an absolute sense but are relevant in relation to the morale of the individuals within the group and their will to continue with their cause. These have been set at parity because when the Afghan statistical variables published by the Brookings Institute are viewed in the aggregate, there is no clear reason to give one group an advantage over the other in this measure (Livingston & O'Hanlon, 2011).

At this point, with the context of the static variables set, the measures of interest in the research questions can be addressed. The level of coordination for this simulation is the measure represented by the variable of the level of coordination between international governmental agents (see Table 1). The effect this attribute has on the simulation is the higher the number the greater the positive impact the international agents have on creating loyalists to the incumbent government when they interact with the population. This in turn increases the number of "patches" that give energy to the government forces and withhold it from the insurgents. The secondary runs were conducted at the extremes of the primary run parameters. These runs were conducted to determine the relative effects of a fifty percent reduction in the initial number of international agents involved in the simulation.

CONCLUSION

The primary runs did not support the null hypothesis; all of the intervention strategies from increasing the level of coordination between military and NGO activities and increasing levels of legitimacy for the indigenous government have a positive effect on the outcomes. Increased levels of violence present in the area of operations, decreased government legitimacy, and lower interagency coordination have a negative impact across the board on the success of the counterinsurgency efforts (see Figure 1). The model successfully emulated the empirical trends on all of these counts and did so in a linear manner with reasonable fidelity as to the scale and proportion described in the case studies.

This particular abstraction was chosen to experiment with concepts such as Provincial Reconstruction Teams in an attempt to determine their effect on the outcomes of counterinsurgency efforts; which were shown to be positive. The second hypothesis, that a "surge" of Western personnel, either military or a combination of military and support personnel, will have a positive impact on security and therefore increase the positive affect engendered in the population by the Western intervention, was however, one area that generated a surprising result that initially appeared counterintuitive.

When the number of international agents was reduced by fifty percent in the simulation, there was a corresponding drop in the probability of a successful counterinsurgency effort; however, the drop was relatively minor in comparison (on average less than ten percent – see Figure 2). This outcome is of interest because the modeled mechanism reflects that of real policy, namely the relatively short period of time the

international forces are present. The average length of time the international agents were active in the simulations was slightly less than one fourth of the time the scenarios took to complete (8.1 out of 32.5 years). In each

Figure 1. Legitimacy and violence level effect on government win probability

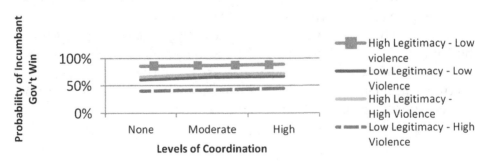

Figure 2. Effects of 50% reduction of international force size

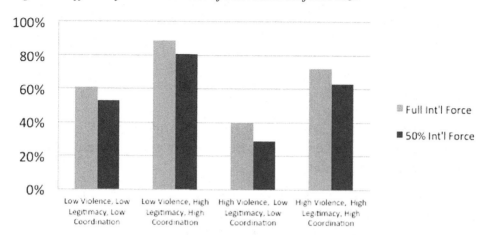

case the international agents set the conditions in which the indigenous agents finished out the simulation.

The concept of a surge can be argued at this point. One of the counter arguments for the manner in which the surge is simulated is that for it to truly reflect the real world effect of a rapid increase in the numbers of Western personnel in the operations area, the model should have those numbers start low and then rapidly build. The answer for this model's design perspective is that each of the model runs begins with all forces in place numerically but at a time that is relative only from the start of the simulation; i.e., the events transpiring up to the point of the simulation beginning are not the focus of the study. Having a scripted start would increase the complexity of the model without changing the parameters of the starting point. The way that such a scripted start would impact the model is if the agents we learning (adapting) as they progressed through the scenario, but as discussed earlier, the timeframes involved and the agent behaviors tending to be ridged with learning taking place upon reflection when hostilities have ended. With the outcomes of the current model, a follow on model including those attributes may be a worthwhile endeavor.

The simulation certainly should not be viewed as supporting the halving of aid delivery or security support. It does however raise the question of priorities of aid delivery and stability assistance. The general observation of de Haan's (2009) that "how much aid is given matters less than how it is given" holds in this particular simulation. A troop surge would not seem to be as impactful as other policy options in the model which raises the issue within real policy applications; notwithstanding the steady parade of senior officials making sweeping statements regarding the success enjoyed due to the surge (yet being rather vague on the specifics causation versus correlation of the successes) (Clinton, 2011).

REFERENCES

ABC News/BBC/ARD. (2010, December 6). *Poll, Afghanistan: Where Things Stand.* Retrieved December 27, 2011, from http://www.langerresearch.com/uploads/1116a1Afghanistan.pdf

Ackerman, S. (2009). *We pay Afghan soldiers less than the Taliban does.* Retrieved December 27, 2011, from http://washingtonindependent.com/70114/we-pay-afghan-soldiers-less-than-the-taliban-does

Barlow, D. (2010). *The Kuwait task force: Post conflict planning and interagency coordination.* Washington, DC: NDU Center for Complex Operations. Retrieved February 4, 2011, from http://www.nps.edu/Academics/AcademicGroups/GPPAG/Documents/PDF/Education%20and%20Research/Research%20Outputs/Case_4_Kuwait_Task_Force.pdf

Barton, F. D. (2010). Setting rule of law priorities in the early days of an intervention. In F. D. Kramer, T. Dempsey, J. Gregoire & S. Merrill (Eds.), *Civil power in irregular conflict* (pp. 149-158). Washington, DC: Center for Naval Analyses, US Army Peacekeeping and Stability Operations Institute and Association of the US Army. Retrieved February 4, 2011, from http://www.cna.org/research/2010/civil-power-irregular-conflict

Brinkerhoff, D. W. (2010). Building resilience in fragile states: The role of governance. In F. D. Kramer, T. Dempsey, J. Gregoire & S. Merrill (Ed.), *Civil power in irregular conflict* (pp. 41 - 49). Washington, DC: Center for Naval Analyses, US Army Peacekeeping and Stability Operations Institute and Association of the US Army. Retrieved February 4, 2011, from http://www.cna.org/research/2010/civil-power-irregular-conflict

Clinton, H. R. (2011). *Testimony before the Senate Foreign Relations Committee.* Retrieved June 28, 2013, from http://www.state.gov/secretary/rm/2011/06/166807.htm

Curry, P. (2010). *Dynamic tension: Security, stability and the opium trade.* Washington, DC: NDU Center for Complex Operations. Retrieved February 4, 2011, from http://www.nps.edu/Academics/AcademicGroups/GPPAG/Documents/PDF/Education%20and%20Research/Research%20Outputs/2_Dynamic_Tension.pdf

de Haan, A. (2009). *How the aid industry works: An introduction to international development.* Sterling, VA: Kumarian Press.

Flanigan, S. (2010). *For the love of god: NGOS and religious identity in a violent world.* Sterling, VA: Kumarian Press.

Galula, D. (1964). *Counterinsurgency warfare: Theory and Practice.* Westport, CT: Praeger Security International.

Gleick, J. (1988). *Chaos: The making of a new science.* New York: Penguin Books.

Guttieri, K. (2010). Interim governments in theory and practice after protracted conflict. In F. D. Kramer, T. Dempsey, J. Gregoire & S. Merrill (Ed.), *Civil power in irregular conflict* (pp. 51 - 56). Washington, DC: Center for Naval Analyses, US Army Peacekeeping and Stability Operations Institute and Association of the US Army. Retrieved February 4, 2011, from http://www.cna.org/research/2010/civil-power-irregular-conflict

Joint Publication 3-07. (2008). Retrieved February 4, 2011, from http://www.dtic.mil/doctrine/new_pubs/jp3_07.pdf

Jones, S. G. (2008). *Counterinsurgency in Afghanistan.* Santa Monica, CA: RAND Corporation.

Kilcullen, D. (2010). *Counterinsurgency redux.* Retrieved December 27, 2011, from http://smallwarsjournal.com/documents/kilcullen1.pdf

Lischer, S. K. (2007). Military intervention and the "force multiplier". *Global Governance, 13,* 99–118.

Livingston, I. S., & O'Hanlon, M. (2011). *Afghanistan index: Tracking variables of reconstruction & security in post-9/11 Afghanistan.* Brookings Institute. Retrieved December 27, 2011, from http://www.brookings.edu/afghanistanindex

Megahan, R. (2010). Achieving immediate developmental change in host-nation police. In F. D. Kramer, T. Dempsey, J. Gregoire & S. Merrill (Ed.), *Civil power in irregular conflict* (pp. 97 - 112). Washington, DC: Center for Naval Analyses, US Army Peacekeeping and Stability Operations Institute and Association of the US Army. Retrieved February 4, 2011, from http://www.cna.org/research/2010/civil-power-irregular-conflict

North, M. J., & Macal, C. M. (2007). *Managing Business Complexity: Discovering Strategic Solutions with Agent-Based Modeling*. New York: Oxford University Press. doi:10.1093/acprof:oso/9780195172119.001.0001

O'Hanlon, M., & Livingston, I. (2011). Prime numbers: A tale of two armies. *Foreign Policy*, (185), 67–73.

Pandya, A. A. (2010). Local and donor obstacles to restoring public administration capacity in the post-conflict societies. In F. D. Kramer, T. Dempsey, J. Gregoire & S. Merrill (Ed.), *Civil power in irregular conflict* (pp. 209-216). Washington, DC: Center for Naval Analyses, US Army Peacekeeping and Stability Operations Institute. Retrieved February 4, 2011, from http://www.cna.org/research/2010/civil-power-irregular-conflict

Pimbo, J. (2010). *Military provision of humanitarian and civic assistance: A day in the life of a civil affairs team in the Horn of Africa*. Washington, DC: NDU Center for Complex Operations. Retrieved February 4, 2011, from http://www.nps.edu/Academics/AcademicGroups/GPPAG/Documents/PDF/Education%20and%20Research/Research%20Outputs/Case_5_Humanitarian_Assistance.pdf

Roberts, N. C. (2010). Spanning bleeding boundaries: Humanitarianism, NGOs, and the civilian-military nexus in the post-cold war era. *Public Administration Review*, *70*(March), 212–222. doi:10.1111/j.1540-6210.2010.02135_2.x

Sepp, K. I. (2005, October). Best practices in counterinsurgency. Military Review, 8-12.

Szayna, T. S., Eaton, D., Barnett, J. E., II, Lawson, B. S., Kelly, T. K., & Haldeman, Z. (2009). *Integrating civilian agencies in stability operations*. Santa Monica, CA: Rand. Retrieved June 19, 2010, from http://www.rand.org/pubs/monographs/2009/RAND_MG801.pdf

United Nations Office on Drugs and Crime. (2011). *Afghanistan opium survey 2011*. Retrieved December 27, 2011, from http://www.unodc.org/documents/cropmonitoring/afghanistan/Executive_Summary_2011_web.pdf von Hippel, K. (2010). Centralized and decentralized governance options after protracted conflict. In F. D. Kramer, T. Dempsey, J. Gregoire & S. Merrill (Eds.), *Civil power in irregular conflict* (pp. 57-66). Washington, DC: Center for Naval Analyses, US Army Peacekeeping and Stability Operations Institute. Retrieved February 4, 2011, from http://www.cna.org/research/2010/civil-power-irregular-conflict

KEY TERMS AND DEFINITIONS

Design Concepts: A standardized way to review the characteristics of an agent-based model.

Initialization: How the model simulation appears at set up; the initial state of the model.

Input: The input data that describe the environmental variables.

Interagency Coordination: The coordination of various governmental and nongovernmental agencies to achieve a desired outcome.

Policy Simulation: The simulation of policy outcomes as it is worked through a series of 'what if' scenarios.

Validation: Addressed whether the model accurately represents the system it is modeling. It answers the question is this the correct model?

Verification: Addresses whether the model programming functions correctly.

Chapter 5
Findings and Conclusion

INTRODUCTION

Many of the findings within the data have generated more questions than answers; but in doing so, illuminated several paths of further investigation that may provide greater insights into the complexities of stabilizing troubled states. This study then, is a starting point on a journey to discover more effective means to deliver humanitarian and development aid to conflicted societies without doing greater harm in the process. Holland (1995) discusses the utility of flight simulators in helping commercial airline pilots experience a variety of scenarios that would be unthinkable to expose passengers to in the real world. The value of the pilot's experience in the simulator, "hinges on the simulator's faithfulness to the aircraft it models" (Holland, 1995, p. 157). With even greater numbers of lives and resources at stake, utilizing agent based modeling as a policy simulator would allow leaders to experiment with numerous response and intervention strategies in a very short period of time. While these simulations may not yield an optimum result, as long as the simulator has strong fidelity to the situation it is modeled for, the simulation outcomes may help prevent an emotional response that only exacerbates versus ameliorating issues in troubled nations. The issue confronting policy makers is, in the words of H. L. Mencken (1880-1956): "For every complex problem, there is a solution that is simple, neat, and wrong" (http://www.watchfuleye.com/mencken.html).

DOI: 10.4018/978-1-5225-1782-5.ch005

PRIMARY RESEACH QUESTION

The research question for this study asked whether increasing coordination among international agents operating in strife ridden societies has a consistent, predictable and positive influence on the success of stability operations. Specifically, does coordination between military forces, international governmental development agencies, and nongovernmental humanitarian relief agencies lead to improved outcomes with regard to the alleviation of human suffering with fewer unintended consequences? The data from the model would seem to indicate otherwise. While there was a generally positive trend to the resultant data, there was not a high degree of consistency presented nor was there sufficient evidence to reject the null hypothesis. While this outcome would appear to lead to a dead end, the qualitative interpretation of the graphical data leads to a new question.

The international agents in the model were generally out of the scenario prior to the conclusion. The new question becomes "are there indicators present within the other indices, such as the relative change in strength of the insurgent versus incumbent government forces or the change in the number of loyalists, which would predict the ultimate outcome of the scenario when the international forces are about to exit?" The current model can readily accommodate such a question by running the simulation one tick at a time. The secondary question that would follow is "what, if any, changes in the international agent contingent has a positive effect on the ultimate outcome of the scenario?" To answer the latter question, a minor degree of modification to the current model would be necessary but within the scope of maintaining a relatively simple model.

The secondary research question concerned the level of violence and the effect that it has on the other variables in the model: namely, does increased incumbent government legitimacy or increased international agent coordination help to offset the deleterious effects of increased violence? Put another way; is it in the best interest of either the incumbent government or the international agents to increase the level of violence (which can be accomplished by simply increasing the number of those respective forces thereby providing additional targets for insurgent activities)? The data suggested a resounding no to that hypothesis. The reverse is actually the case. It is in the best interest of the insurgent to increase the level of violence within the scenario. While a surge of operational international forces intuitively makes sense, it is also intuitive that an escalation of violence serves to undermine the legitimacy of the incumbent government. The less legitimacy the incumbent government has, the less it has to lose by increasing violence relative to a more legitimate incumbent government. However, in both cases, the probability of a successful outcome is dramatically reduced.

On the other hand, if the level of violence can be kept low, increases in legitimacy for the incumbent government has a favorable impact on the prospects of a win for the incumbent government. The difficulty with this reality is that if the insurgents are not interested in making peace, they also have a say in how violent the struggle becomes. The insurgent leaders would not require a sophisticated intelligence gathering apparatus to determine that as they increase attacks and the level of violence, the legitimacy of the incumbent government suffers. The trick for the insurgent leadership is to avoid having public opinion turn on them which is why their selection of targets for violence is critical (Galula, 1964).

The level of violence did have a surprisingly consistent effect on the amount of time the simulation took to run to completion. As the level of violence increased, the amount of time it took to determine a winner dropped significantly. Once again, when determining a course of action, the amount of time relative to how long international forces can expect to be deployed can be predicted based upon the level of violence of the insurgency. Unfortunately, while the outcomes may be determined sooner rather than later, the type of outcome becomes less stable and frequently less favorable. These findings lead to the following observations on future research.

FUTURE RESEARCH

One of the most pressing questions generated from this research is "are there indicators present within the other indices, such as the relative change in strength of the insurgent versus incumbent government forces or the change in the number of loyalists, which would predict the ultimate outcome of the scenario when the international forces are about to exit?" By continuing with this model and running it one tick at a time it may be possible to identify the critical elements within the latent variables that predict the outcome of a given scenario. By examining the graphic interface and observing and recording the status of the interface with regard to the trending of the number of loyalists, incumbent government agents, and insurgent agents, there may be identifiable patterns that emerge and provide insight into the critical elements determining the outcome.

Some of the critical areas for observation are the relative distribution of loyalists versus insurgent sympathizers (which are referred to in NetLogo as patches) within the graphic. Qualitatively, the distribution of these patches within the scenario environment is related to the eventual outcome. Generally, if the insurgent sympathizers are relatively evenly distributed throughout the environment, the insurgent agents have defeated the incumbent government agents. If the insurgent sympathizers are lumped together (concentrated in one area), the incumbent government has carried the day. The critical question becomes "are these distributions of patches related to the outcomes in a statistically significant manner?" Also, if the distribution of the patches is in fact positively associated with the outcome, then does the outcome cause the shape of the distribution or does the distribution influence the outcome? This cause and effect would be most readily determined by timing. If the distribution of the various types of patches begins to take its final form early in the scenario, then the hypothesis would be that the distribution is driving the outcome. If the distribution does not take its final shape until late in the scenario, or if it changes late in the scenario, then the cause and effect is reversed.

This initial step significantly helps to drive the remaining branches and sequels of the research. If the shape of the distribution of the patches influences the scenario outcome, then what factors affect that distribution? If the international agents and incumbent government agents allow for a safe haven within a given area, will that shape the distribution of the insurgent sympathizers within the scenario? Is it possible to influence the outcome of an insurgency with a tactic as simple as allowing an escape for the insurgent agents? If this is not the case, then what factors help determine the distribution of the insurgent sympathizers? Are there any activities conducted by the international agents that influence the shape of the distribution? All of these questions are relevant to the policy decisions made with regard to how best to conduct the stability operations in the troubled state.

Once those critical elements have been identified, it is then much more straightforward to redesign the model to identify the interrelationships of these elements. Again, the ability to run scenarios and observe a graphic interface in agent based modeling provides an optimal tool for this type of research. It is also very helpful to be able to isolate changes within the scenario to identify the variable(s) that are driving the observed emergent behavior. Finally, having a graphic interface is helpful in presenting data to audiences that may not be expert in the field of agent based modeling or working with latent variables. The ability to observe a phenomenon as it unfolds reinforces the narrative of the research presentation and helps the audience make intuitive sense of the outcome.

POLICY IMPLICATIONS

For policy makers, the outcomes of this research are cautionary. To paraphrase Benjamin Valentino (2011), the question for the international community boils down to whether humanitarian intervention can work. The answer to that question is representative of most issues within international relations. The available options fall along a continuum of poor choices. The one extreme is the use of heavy handed military intervention by international forces. Coalitions of allies, utilizing brute force to stop humanitarian outrages perpetrated by incumbent regime despots, rarely obtain optimal outcomes. Using the primarily military intervention in Somalia, a country with a population of roughly eight and one half million people, the United States alone spent over seven billion dollars. The calculus for the number of lives saved was between ten thousand and twenty-five thousand which means the United States spent between two hundred and eighty to seven hundred thousand dollars for each life saved (Valentino 2011, p. 67). The military heavy option for humanitarian interventions is notoriously high in terms of monetary costs as well as the risk of friction with allies and the possible loss of life on the part of the intercessors. But even the seemingly benign action of providing development aid has caused major problems. The June 2011 Senate Foreign Relations Committee report contained the following admission:

Foreign aid, when misspent, can fuel corruption, distort labor and goods markets, undermine the host government's ability to exert control over resources, and contribute to insecurity. According to the World Bank, an estimated 97 percent of Afghanistan's gross domestic product (GDP) is derived from spending related to the international military and donor community presence. Afghanistan could suffer a severe economic depression when foreign troops leave in 2014 unless the proper planning begins now. (p. 2)

Sara Lischer (2007) has put forward solid arguments that caution policy makers on the use of humanitarian soldiers as a force multiplier. According to Lischer, many military planners now include providing humanitarian assistance as part of their strategic plan to win the hearts and minds of the target population. The problem is that such uses of military forces do not substitute for the provision of traditional security forces to stabilize an area. In fact the opposite can be true, which was borne out in the outcomes of the simulations with the coordinating of international agent forces. Utilizing military forces for the provision of humanitarian aid, particularly as part of a plan for the achievement of strategic objectives, can endanger the civilian nongovernmental organization personnel that are attempting to provide humanitarian assistance within the same operational space (Lischer, 2007). Nancy Roberts (2010) provides amplifying support to Lischer's position in what she describes as domain conflict.

Roberts describes "bleeding boundaries" in the roles and domains between civilian nongovernmental organizations and military forces in the delivery of humanitarian aid. Both Roberts and Lischer concur that when military forces are used in a logistical capacity such as providing airlift support for the movement of supplies and refugees following a natural disaster, there is little to no domain conflict. The nongovernmental organizations do not feel pressure on their core values, or guiding principles of neutrality, impartiality, and independence. This circumstance is confirmed by the outcomes of the model runs conducted within this research project. With high levels of international coordination and cooperation, and low levels of violence, the probability of the incumbent government recovering and maintaining or regaining control of governance within its borders is very high; greater than eighty-six percent. The problem becomes that the success of the international community intervention comes at the expense of undermining the legitimacy of the incumbent government. If the beginning level of legitimacy of the incumbent government is high, the probability of a successful outcome for that government is reduced by up to ten percent. This is one of the more unexpected and confounding issues that emerged from this research that makes the options for policy makers even less clear.

The situation becomes even more vexing as the level of violence begins to increase. Lischer (2005) also points out the difficulties in attempting a civilian only humanitarian response in dealing with despotism. Her treatise in this circumstance is that the provision of aid is never neutral. There are consequences to attempting to provide aid to either internally or externally displaced populations. Attempting to provide aid to internally displaced refugees can fall into the trap of aiding the corrupt government that is causing the dislocation in the first place. An example is the problems the international efforts ran into attempting to help the victims of Cyclone Nargis in Myanmar. The Myanmar government insisted that all aid was seen by the people to be delivered through the government. This insistence caused critical supplies to languish in warehouses awaiting government approved transportation. The problems became severe enough that there were voices in the international community calling for the use of military force to get relief supplies to victims of the cyclone (Roman & Thein, 2010). But these issues pale in comparison to the problems encountered in delivering humanitarian aid to externally displaced refugees.

Lischer (2005) lists numerous examples of humanitarian efforts that exacerbate an unstable and volatile situation. One she lists that was the most relevant to this research is the case of Afghanistan. The provision of aid by the international community during the Soviet occupation of Afghanistan enabled the emergence and solidification of the Taliban as an insurgent force fighting against the occupation. The humanitarian aid was controlled by the leaders of the Afghan refugees and enabled them to gain power and authority within the camps in Pakistan. From this base of authority, the leaders were able to form an insurgent force that could leave the safe haven of the camps to fight, knowing their families were safe, and then return for rest and recuperation (Lischer, 2005). This situation was exacerbated by the United States funneling of arms to the refugees which militarized the camps to an even greater extent and ultimately led to the insurgent success against the Soviets. The question then is where upon this continuum does the correct policy balance lie? While this research in no way provides a road map of what precise policy steps to take, it does point to some items for consideration when contemplating humanitarian and / or stability operations within an unstable nation or population.

POLICY CONSIDERATION RECOMMENDATIONS

One of the primary outputs generated from this research is the uncertainty of a positive outcome resulting from international intervention in the affairs of a troubled nation. This result is not unexpected given the complexity of the issues that swirl around international relations. The surprising result was the increase in complexity highlighted by such a simple agent based model. The overarching question for policy makers is what items should be considered when weighing the risks of intervention anywhere along the continuum of options previously outlined? This concluding section suggests a few additions to the numerous considerations for policy makers involved in such deliberations.

CONCLUSION

In Barbara Tuchman's seminal work, *The March of Folly* (1984), she lists three attributes of folly that are defined as the pursuit of policy by governments that are counter to their self-interests. The first is that "it must be perceived as counter-productive in its own time, not merely by hindsight" (Tuchman,

1984, p. 5). Since the scope of her writing covered vast periods of history, this rule is critical to avoid the curse of hindsight. The second attribute of folly is "a feasible alternative course of action must have been available" and third, "the policy in question should be that of a group, not an individual ruler, and should persist beyond any one political lifetime" (Tuchman, 1984, p. 5). In an effort to provide the questions to help avoid meeting these three interlocks, the first and obvious question is whether the proposed action is in the collective best interest. This consideration makes the list only because it is so obvious; an attempt to carry on a discussion without mentioning it is pointless. For the most part, this question is probably the most thoroughly debated. The problem usually does not stem from the initial decision, the issue comes from the reluctance to change course when events are not aligning with expectations. The impulse to throw good money after bad, and continue down a path counter to self-interest is known in accounting as confusing sunk costs with future costs. Resources that have been expended cannot be recovered. The decision of whether to continue the current course of action should be based upon future costs; the sunk costs, no matter how large, should not enter into the decision matrix. The need to continuously reevaluate circumstances and events should be treated as an imperative, not a sign of weakness or indecision.

The next item is the examination of what the end state looks like when the intervention is complete. If there is an effort to establish a western style democracy in a country that has only known feudal or autocratic rule throughout its history, there is a high probability of a mismatch between the change capacity of the society and the desired end state of the intervening agency. This circumstance sets up a very difficult path with an uncertain outcome due to the probable need for a large number of resources to effect the desired change and the level of resistance generated. Such a scenario falls into the outcome domain of this research as high violence, low incumbent government legitimacy, and high levels of coordination (the best possible set up for this scenario). This yields only a seventy-three percent favorable outcome percentage and that is if the international agents involved do everything in a coordinated and cooperative fashion. Otherwise the percentage drops to thirty-three. Once again, is there an alternative outcome that the international community can accept that will be more aligned with the change capacity of the society in question? Tuchman sounds prescient when discussing such miscalculations throughout history when she states, "This curious vacuum of understanding came from what may be called cultural ignorance, a frequent component of folly" (Tuchman, 1984, p. 31).

But do world leaders periodically wake up one morning and suddenly decide to ignore their own best interests and those of their countrymen and knowingly engage in counterproductive interventions in sovereign nations? The operative word in such a question is "knowingly." As we have previously discussed, complex systems contain multiple feedback loops and cause and effect relationships that can be widely displaced either temporally, spatially, or both. An action that seems intuitive upon the first examination of a situation can turn out to be the antithesis of what the correct course of action should have been. Given the complexity of these issues, coupled with the multiple feedback loops and widely separate cause and effect relationships, the probability of downside outcomes may be beyond the capacity of humans to calculate. Considering this in advance may be the key to avoid joining Tuchman's march of folly.

REFERENCES

Galula, D. (1964). *Counterinsurgency warfare: Theory and Practice.* Westport, CT: Praeger Security International.

Holland, J. H. (1995). *Hidden order: How adaptation builds complexity.* Reading, MA: Helix Books.

Lischer, S. K. (2005). *Dangerous sanctuaries: Refugee camps, civil war, and the dilemmas of humanitarian aid.* Ithaca, NY: Cornell University Press.

Lischer, S. K. (2007). Military intervention and the "force multiplier.". *Global Governance, 13,* 99–118.

Mencken, H. L. (1880 – 1956). *Quotes From H. L. Mencken* (B. MacLeod, Ed.). Retrieved February 26, 2012, from http://www.watchfuleye.com/mencken.html

Roman, O., & Thein, Y. E. (2010). *Getting help to victims of 2008 cyclone Nargis: AmeriCares engages with Myanmar's military government sequel. The Kennedy School Case Program, case number 1931.1.* Cambridge, MA: John F. Kennedy School of Government, Harvard University.

Tuchman, B. W. (1984). *The march of folly.* New York: Alfred A. Knopf, Inc.

United States Senate Committee on Foreign Relations. (2011). *Evaluating U.S. Foreign Assistance to Afghanistan.* Washington, DC: Author.

Valentino, B. A. (2011). The true cost of humanitarian intervention: The hard truth about a noble notion. *Foreign Affairs*, *90*(6), 60–73.

KEY TERMS AND DEFINITIONS

Branches: Or branch plans; the planning options that become active when strategic decision points have been reached in an operation.

Complexity: The environment or human interaction. Cause and effect can be widely separated temporally, spatially, or both. Human agents behave unpredictably because their motivations are typically not clear to decision makers.

Folly: The pursuit of policy by governments that are counter to their self-interests.

Future Costs: The long-term, ongoing costs that are incurred from a course of action.

Sequels: The sub-plans that that follow branch plans, usually general in nature.

Sunk Costs: Costs that have occurred in the past and are unrecoverable. These costs should not be considered in future courses of action, but frequently are.

Uncertainty: The opacity that clouds decision making in complex environments. Cause and effect are unclear.

Related Readings

To continue IGI Global's long-standing tradition of advancing innovation through emerging research, please find below a compiled list of recommended IGI Global book chapters and journal articles in the areas of natural disasters, emergency management, and crisis response. These related readings will provide additional information and guidance to further enrich your knowledge and assist you with your own research.

Adams, T. (2014). An Examination of Challenges Faced by First Responders in the Midst of Disaster. In C. Brown, K. Peters, & K. Nyarko (Eds.), *Cases on Research and Knowledge Discovery: Homeland Security Centers of Excellence* (pp. 198–216). Hershey, PA: IGI Global. doi:10.4018/978-1-4666-5946-9.ch009

Adler, M. (2015). Floods Monitoring. In C. Maftei (Ed.), *Extreme Weather and Impacts of Climate Change on Water Resources in the Dobrogea Region* (pp. 312–344). Hershey, PA: IGI Global. doi:10.4018/978-1-4666-8438-6.ch011

Akaichi, J., & Mhadhbi, L. (2016). A Clinical Decision Support System: Ontology-Driven Approach for Effective Emergency Management. In J. Moon & M. Galea (Eds.), *Improving Health Management through Clinical Decision Support Systems* (pp. 270–294). Hershey, PA: IGI Global. doi:10.4018/978-1-4666-9432-3.ch013

Almagrabi, A., Loke, S. W., & Torabi, T. (2014). Spatial Relations in Contextual Information for Mobile Emergency Messaging. In B. Guo, D. Riboni, & P. Hu (Eds.), *Creating Personal, Social, and Urban Awareness through Pervasive Computing* (pp. 274–298). Hershey, PA: IGI Global. doi:10.4018/978-1-4666-4695-7.ch012

Related Readings

Anderson, L. R. (2017). Assessing the Interactions between Native American Tribes and the U.S. Government in Homeland Security and Emergency Management Policy. In M. Dawson, D. Kisku, P. Gupta, J. Sing, & W. Li (Eds.), *Developing Next-Generation Countermeasures for Homeland Security Threat Prevention* (pp. 51–71). Hershey, PA: IGI Global. doi:10.4018/978-1-5225-0703-1.ch003

Andersson, D. (2014). An Externalizable Model of Tactical Mission Control for Knowledge Transfer. *International Journal of Information Systems for Crisis Response and Management, 6*(3), 16–37. doi:10.4018/IJISCRAM.2014070102

Annunziato, A., Doherty, B., & Khanh, H. (2014). A Modular Collaborative Web-Based Framework for Humanitarian Crisis Management. In Z. Mahmood (Ed.), *IT in the Public Sphere: Applications in Administration, Government, Politics, and Planning* (pp. 18–46). Hershey, PA: IGI Global. doi:10.4018/978-1-4666-4719-0.ch002

Anwar, J. (2015). Reproductive and Mental Health during Natural Disaster: Implications and Issues for Women in Developing Nations – A Case Example. In M. Sheikh, A. Mahamoud, & M. Househ (Eds.), *Transforming Public Health in Developing Nations* (pp. 265–291). Hershey, PA: IGI Global. doi:10.4018/978-1-4666-8702-8.ch012

Arbanas, S. M., & Arbanas, Ž. (2015). Landslides: A Guide to Researching Landslide Phenomena and Processes. In N. Gaurina-Medjimurec (Ed.), *Handbook of Research on Advancements in Environmental Engineering* (pp. 474–510). Hershey, PA: IGI Global. doi:10.4018/978-1-4666-7336-6.ch017

Arias-Hernandez, R., & Fisher, B. (2014). Designing Visual Analytic Tools for Emergency Operation Centers: A Qualitative Approach. *International Journal of Information Systems for Crisis Response and Management, 6*(3), 1–15. doi:10.4018/IJISCRAM.2014070101

Arlikatti, S., Kendra, J., & Jennings, E. (2015). Corporate Social Responsibility in Enhancing Disaster Education. In M. Hamner, S. Stovall, D. Taha, & S. Brahimi (Eds.), *Emergency Management and Disaster Response Utilizing Public-Private Partnerships* (pp. 183–194). Hershey, PA: IGI Global. doi:10.4018/978-1-4666-8159-0.ch010

Attia, S., Boubetra, A., & Saoud, M. S. (2016). Development of an Emergency Response Management using Mobile Devices for Hospital Infrastructures Affected by Power Grid Failures. *International Journal of Healthcare Information Systems and Informatics, 11*(1), 36–57. doi:10.4018/IJHISI.2016010103

Bahinipati, C. S., Patnaik, U., & Viswanathan, P. K. (2016). What Causes Economic Losses from Natural Disasters in India? In S. Dinda (Ed.), *Handbook of Research on Climate Change Impact on Health and Environmental Sustainability* (pp. 157–175). Hershey, PA: IGI Global. doi:10.4018/978-1-4666-8814-8.ch008

Bahir, E., & Peled, A. (2015). Keyword Selection Methodology for Identification of Major Events using Social Networks. *International Journal of Information Systems for Crisis Response and Management*, 7(1), 42–60. doi:10.4018/IJISCRAM.2015010103

Baker, W. (2016). Responding to High-Volume Water Disasters in the Research Library Context. In E. Decker & J. Townes (Eds.), *Handbook of Research on Disaster Management and Contingency Planning in Modern Libraries* (pp. 282–310). Hershey, PA: IGI Global. doi:10.4018/978-1-4666-8624-3.ch013

Balogun, O., & Tetteh, E. G. (2015). Data Fusion Aiding Tool (DAFAT) Design for Emergency Command and Control Using Lean Principles. In E. Tetteh & B. Uzochukwu (Eds.), *Lean Six Sigma Approaches in Manufacturing, Services, and Production* (pp. 202–230). Hershey, PA: IGI Global. doi:10.4018/978-1-4666-7320-5.ch008

Baroni, P., Fogli, D., Giacomin, M., Guida, G., Provenza, L. P., Rossi, M., & Žnidaršič, M. et al. (2014). A Participatory Approach to Designing Decision Support Systems in Emergency Management. *International Journal of Decision Support System Technology*, 6(1), 60–80. doi:10.4018/ijdsst.2014010104

Barthe-Delanoë, A., Carbonnel, S., Bénaben, F., & Pingaud, H. (2014). An Event-Driven Platform for Agility Management of Crisis Response. *International Journal of Information Systems for Crisis Response and Management*, 6(2), 54–70. doi:10.4018/ijiscram.2014040104

Basu, J. P. (2016). Coastal Poverty, Resource-Dependent Livelihood, Climate Change, and Adaptation: An Empirical Study in Indian Coastal Sunderbans. In S. Dinda (Ed.), *Handbook of Research on Climate Change Impact on Health and Environmental Sustainability* (pp. 441–454). Hershey, PA: IGI Global. doi:10.4018/978-1-4666-8814-8.ch022

Behnam, B. (2017). Simulating Post-Earthquake Fire Loading in Conventional RC Structures. In P. Samui, S. Chakraborty, & D. Kim (Eds.), *Modeling and Simulation Techniques in Structural Engineering* (pp. 425–444). Hershey, PA: IGI Global. doi:10.4018/978-1-5225-0588-4.ch015

Related Readings

Behnassi, M., Kahime, K., Boussaa, S., Boumezzough, A., & Messouli, M. (2017). Infectious Diseases and Climate Vulnerability in Morocco: Governance and Adaptation Options. In M. Bouzid (Ed.), *Examining the Role of Environmental Change on Emerging Infectious Diseases and Pandemics* (pp. 138–162). Hershey, PA: IGI Global. doi:10.4018/978-1-5225-0553-2.ch006

Bender, S. R. (2016). Floodplain Infrastructure and the Toxic Tide. In A. McKeown & G. Bugyi (Eds.), *Impact of Water Pollution on Human Health and Environmental Sustainability* (pp. 150–173). Hershey, PA: IGI Global. doi:10.4018/978-1-4666-9559-7.ch007

Berndt, H., Mentler, T., & Herczeg, M. (2015). Optical Head-Mounted Displays in Mass Casualty Incidents: Keeping an Eye on Patients and Hazardous Materials. *International Journal of Information Systems for Crisis Response and Management*, 7(3), 1–15. doi:10.4018/IJISCRAM.2015070101

Bimonte, S., Boucelma, O., Machabert, O., & Sellami, S. (2014). A Generic Spatial OLAP Model for Evaluating Natural Hazards in a Volunteered Geographic Information Context. *International Journal of Agricultural and Environmental Information Systems*, 5(4), 40–55. doi:10.4018/ijaeis.2014100102

Boersma, K., Diks, D., Ferguson, J., & Wolbers, J. (2016). From Reactive to Proactive Use of Social Media in Emergency Response: A Critical Discussion of the Twitcident Project. In G. Silvius (Ed.), *Strategic Integration of Social Media into Project Management Practice* (pp. 236–252). Hershey, PA: IGI Global. doi:10.4018/978-1-4666-9867-3.ch014

Bouzid, M. (2017). Waterborne Diseases and Climate Change: Impact and Implications. In M. Bouzid (Ed.), *Examining the Role of Environmental Change on Emerging Infectious Diseases and Pandemics* (pp. 89–108). Hershey, PA: IGI Global. doi:10.4018/978-1-5225-0553-2.ch004

Bowers, M., & Cherne, G. (2015). A Lessons Framework for Civil-Military-Police Conflict and Disaster Management: An Australian Perspective. In S. McIntyre, K. Dalkir, P. Paul, & I. Kitimbo (Eds.), *Utilizing Evidence-Based Lessons Learned for Enhanced Organizational Innovation and Change* (pp. 152–171). Hershey, PA: IGI Global. doi:10.4018/978-1-4666-6453-1.ch008

Bowles, D. C. (2017). Climate Change-Associated Conflict and Infectious Disease. In M. Bouzid (Ed.), *Examining the Role of Environmental Change on Emerging Infectious Diseases and Pandemics* (pp. 68–88). Hershey, PA: IGI Global. doi:10.4018/978-1-5225-0553-2.ch003

Brengarth, L. B., Mujkic, E., & Millar, M. A. (2015). Social Media in Crisis: How Social Media Created a NPO and Relief during a Wildfire Crisis. In H. Asencio & R. Sun (Eds.), *Cases on Strategic Social Media Utilization in the Nonprofit Sector* (pp. 1–23). Hershey, PA: IGI Global. doi:10.4018/978-1-4666-8188-0.ch001

Cai, T. (2014). Geospatial Technology-Based E-Government Design for Environmental Protection and Emergency Response. In K. Bwalya (Ed.), *Technology Development and Platform Enhancements for Successful Global E-Government Design* (pp. 157–184). Hershey, PA: IGI Global. doi:10.4018/978-1-4666-4900-2.ch009

Carmicheal, D. W. (2016). The Incident Command System: Applying Emergency Response Best Practice to Your Disaster. In E. Decker & J. Townes (Eds.), *Handbook of Research on Disaster Management and Contingency Planning in Modern Libraries* (pp. 25–48). Hershey, PA: IGI Global. doi:10.4018/978-1-4666-8624-3.ch002

Carvalho, T., Santos, L. B., Luz, E. F., Ishibashi, R., Jorge, A. A., & Londe, L. R. (2016). An Open Source Approach for Watersheds Delimitation to Support Flood Monitoring. *International Journal of Distributed Systems and Technologies*, 7(4), 77–88. doi:10.4018/IJDST.2016100105

Chandler, T., & Beedasy, J. (2015). mLearning to Enhance Disaster Preparedness Education in K-12 Schools. In H. An, S. Alon, & D. Fuentes (Eds.) Tablets in K-12 Education: Integrated Experiences and Implications (pp. 75-89). Hershey, PA: IGI Global. doi:10.4018/978-1-4666-6300-8.ch006

Chandler, T., Crocco, M., & Marri, A. R. (2014). Systems Thinking about Severe Storms in Social Studies Education. In K. Thomas & H. Muga (Eds.), *Handbook of Research on Pedagogical Innovations for Sustainable Development* (pp. 348–367). Hershey, PA: IGI Global. doi:10.4018/978-1-4666-5856-1.ch016

Chapman, J., Davis, L. B., Samanlioglu, F., & Qu, X. (2014). Evaluating the Effectiveness of Pre-Positioning Policies in Response to Natural Disasters. *International Journal of Operations Research and Information Systems*, 5(2), 86–100. doi:10.4018/ijoris.2014040105

Chatterjee, T., & Dinda, S. (2016). Climate Change, Human Health and Some Economic Issues. In S. Dinda (Ed.), *Handbook of Research on Climate Change Impact on Health and Environmental Sustainability* (pp. 26–41). Hershey, PA: IGI Global. doi:10.4018/978-1-4666-8814-8.ch002

Chaudron, G. (2016). After the Flood: Lessons Learned from Small-Scale Disasters. In E. Decker & J. Townes (Eds.), *Handbook of Research on Disaster Management and Contingency Planning in Modern Libraries* (pp. 389–411). Hershey, PA: IGI Global. doi:10.4018/978-1-4666-8624-3.ch017

Chin, S. (2016). Surviving Sandy: Recovering Collections after a Natural Disaster. In E. Decker & J. Townes (Eds.), *Handbook of Research on Disaster Management and Contingency Planning in Modern Libraries* (pp. 366–388). Hershey, PA: IGI Global. doi:10.4018/978-1-4666-8624-3.ch016

Chtourou, W., & Bouzguenda, L. (2015). Interaction Protocols Adaptation Based Coordination for Crisis Management Processes. *International Journal of Information Systems for Crisis Response and Management, 7*(4), 67–87. doi:10.4018/IJISCRAM.2015100104

Chun, S. A., & Artigas, F. (2015). Participatory Environmental Planning Platform. In C. Silva (Ed.), *Emerging Issues, Challenges, and Opportunities in Urban E-Planning* (pp. 46–68). Hershey, PA: IGI Global. doi:10.4018/978-1-4666-8150-7.ch003

Çinal, H., Taşkan, Ş., & Baybaş, F. (2015). Dynamic Disaster Coordination System with Web based Html5 API. *International Journal of 3-D Information Modeling (IJ3DIM), 4*(2), 1-15. doi:10.4018/IJ3DIM.2015040101

Confalonieri, U., Menezes, J. A., & Margonari, C. (2017). Environmental Change and the Emergence of Infectious Diseases: A Regional Perspective from South America. In M. Bouzid (Ed.), *Examining the Role of Environmental Change on Emerging Infectious Diseases and Pandemics* (pp. 109–137). Hershey, PA: IGI Global. doi:10.4018/978-1-5225-0553-2.ch005

Corbett, J. M., Brennan, S., & Whitely, A. (2016). Harnessing the Chaotic: Using the Participatory Geoweb to Make Sense of Forest Fires. *International Journal of E-Planning Research, 5*(3), 27–41. doi:10.4018/IJEPR.2016070103

Cowick, C., & Cowick, J. (2016). Planning for a Disaster: Effective Emergency Management in the 21st Century. In E. Decker & J. Townes (Eds.), *Handbook of Research on Disaster Management and Contingency Planning in Modern Libraries* (pp. 49–69). Hershey, PA: IGI Global. doi:10.4018/978-1-4666-8624-3.ch003

Cruz-Cantillo, Y. (2014). A System Dynamics Approach to Humanitarian Logistics and the Transportation of Relief Supplies. *International Journal of System Dynamics Applications, 3*(3), 96–126. doi:10.4018/ijsda.2014070105

Curran, S. J. (2015). Application of Cellular Communications Models and Designs for Use in Disaster-Aftermath Related Scenarios. *International Journal of Interdisciplinary Telecommunications and Networking, 7*(3), 46–56. doi:10.4018/IJITN.2015070104

Das, S. (2016). Health Impact of Water-Related Diseases in Developing Countries on Account of Climate Change – A Systematic Review: A Study in Regard to South Asian Countries. In S. Dinda (Ed.), *Handbook of Research on Climate Change Impact on Health and Environmental Sustainability* (pp. 42–60). Hershey, PA: IGI Global. doi:10.4018/978-1-4666-8814-8.ch003

Deenapanray, P. N., & Ramma, I. (2015). Adaptations to Climate Change and Climate Variability in the Agriculture Sector in Mauritius: Lessons from a Technical Needs Assessment. In W. Ganpat & W. Isaac (Eds.), *Impacts of Climate Change on Food Security in Small Island Developing States* (pp. 130–165). Hershey, PA: IGI Global. doi:10.4018/978-1-4666-6501-9.ch005

Dervisevic, S. (2017). Emergence of the Ebola Virus Disease in West Africa. In M. Bouzid (Ed.), *Examining the Role of Environmental Change on Emerging Infectious Diseases and Pandemics* (pp. 163–177). Hershey, PA: IGI Global. doi:10.4018/978-1-5225-0553-2.ch007

Detjen, H., Hoffmann, S., Rösner, L., Winter, S., Geisler, S., Krämer, N., & Bumiller, G. (2015). Integrating Volunteers into Rescue Processes: Analysis of User Requirements and Mobile App Conception. *International Journal of Information Systems for Crisis Response and Management*, 7(2), 1–18. doi:10.4018/IJISCRAM.2015040101

Dixon, J., & Abashian, N. (2016). Beyond the Collection: Emergency Planning for Public and Staff Safety. In E. Decker & J. Townes (Eds.), *Handbook of Research on Disaster Management and Contingency Planning in Modern Libraries* (pp. 120–140). Hershey, PA: IGI Global. doi:10.4018/978-1-4666-8624-3.ch006

Egan, J., & Anderson, T. (2015). Considerations for a Model of Public-Private Sector Collaboration in the Provision of Disaster Relief: Incentives and Limits. In M. Hamner, S. Stovall, D. Taha, & S. Brahimi (Eds.), *Emergency Management and Disaster Response Utilizing Public-Private Partnerships* (pp. 1–15). Hershey, PA: IGI Global. doi:10.4018/978-1-4666-8159-0.ch001

Ekker, K. (2015). Emergency Management Training and Social Network Analysis: Providing Experiential Data for Virtual Responders. In T. Issa & P. Isaías (Eds.), *Artificial Intelligence Technologies and the Evolution of Web 3.0* (pp. 273–289). Hershey, PA: IGI Global. doi:10.4018/978-1-4666-8147-7.ch013

Ellebrecht, N., & Kaufmann, S. (2014). Boosting Efficiency Through the Use Of IT?: Reconfiguring the Management of Mass Casualty Incidents in Germany. *International Journal of Information Systems for Crisis Response and Management*, 6(4), 1–18. doi:10.4018/IJISCRAM.2014100101

Related Readings

Erskine, M. A., & Pepper, W. (2015). Enhancing Emergency Response Management using Emergency Description Information Technology (EDIT): A Design Science Approach. *International Journal of Electronic Government Research, 11*(2), 51–65. doi:10.4018/IJEGR.2015040104

Eudoxie, G. D., & Wuddivira, M. (2015). Soil, Water, and Agricultural Adaptations. In W. Ganpat & W. Isaac (Eds.), *Impacts of Climate Change on Food Security in Small Island Developing States* (pp. 255–279). Hershey, PA: IGI Global. doi:10.4018/978-1-4666-6501-9.ch009

Ford, J. L., Stephens, K. K., & Ford, J. S. (2014). Digital Restrictions at Work: Exploring How Selectively Exclusive Policies Affect Crisis Communication. *International Journal of Information Systems for Crisis Response and Management, 6*(4), 19–28. doi:10.4018/IJISCRAM.2014100102

Galloup, A. (2016). One Plan, Four Libraries: A Case Study in Disaster Planning for a Four-Campus Academic Institution. In E. Decker & J. Townes (Eds.), *Handbook of Research on Disaster Management and Contingency Planning in Modern Libraries* (pp. 166–183). Hershey, PA: IGI Global. doi:10.4018/978-1-4666-8624-3.ch008

Gao, T., & Rong, L. (2014). Study on Management of the Life Cycle of Emergency Plan System Based on Effectiveness. *International Journal of Knowledge and Systems Science, 5*(1), 49–64. doi:10.4018/ijkss.2014010105

Garrido, S., & Nicoletti, J. (2017). First Responder Psychological Recovery Following a Mass Casualty Event. In C. Mitchell & E. Dorian (Eds.), *Police Psychology and Its Growing Impact on Modern Law Enforcement* (pp. 143–157). Hershey, PA: IGI Global. doi:10.4018/978-1-5225-0813-7.ch007

Gasmelseid, T. M. (2014). Improving Emergency Response Systems Through the Use of Intelligent Information Systems. *International Journal of Intelligent Information Technologies, 10*(2), 37–55. doi:10.4018/ijiit.2014040103

Hallberg, N., Hallberg, J., Granlund, H., & Woltjer, R. (2014). Exploring the Rationale for Emergency Management Information Systems for Local Communities. *International Journal of Information Systems for Crisis Response and Management, 6*(2), 16–37. doi:10.4018/ijiscram.2014040102

Halliru, S. L. (2017). Climate Change Effects on Human Health with a Particular Focus on Vector-Borne Diseases and Malaria in Africa: A Case Study from Kano State, Nigeria Investigating Perceptions about Links between Malaria Epidemics, Weather Variables, and Climate Change. In M. Bouzid (Ed.), *Examining the Role of Environmental Change on Emerging Infectious Diseases and Pandemics* (pp. 205–229). Hershey, PA: IGI Global. doi:10.4018/978-1-5225-0553-2.ch009

Hamilton, R., & Brown, D. (2016). Disaster Management and Continuity Planning in Libraries: Changes since the Year 2000. In E. Decker & J. Townes (Eds.), *Handbook of Research on Disaster Management and Contingency Planning in Modern Libraries* (pp. 1–24). Hershey, PA: IGI Global. doi:10.4018/978-1-4666-8624-3.ch001

Hamner, M. (2015). Closing the Gaps in Public Private Partnerships in Emergency Management: A Gap Analysis. In M. Hamner, S. Stovall, D. Taha, & S. Brahimi (Eds.), *Emergency Management and Disaster Response Utilizing Public-Private Partnerships* (pp. 64–97). Hershey, PA: IGI Global. doi:10.4018/978-1-4666-8159-0.ch005

Harris, E. N. (2015). A Public Sector Practitioner's Perspective on Public Private Partnerships. In M. Hamner, S. Stovall, D. Taha, & S. Brahimi (Eds.), *Emergency Management and Disaster Response Utilizing Public-Private Partnerships* (pp. 54–63). Hershey, PA: IGI Global. doi:10.4018/978-1-4666-8159-0.ch004

Hassanzadeh, R., & Nedovic-Budic, Z. (2014). Assessment of the Contribution of Crowd Sourced Data to Post-Earthquake Building Damage Detection. *International Journal of Information Systems for Crisis Response and Management*, 6(1), 1–37. doi:10.4018/ijiscram.2014010101

Hawe, G. I., Coates, G., Wilson, D. T., & Crouch, R. S. (2015). Improving Agent-Based Simulation of Major Incident Response in the United Kingdom through Conceptual and Operational Validation. *International Journal of Information Systems for Crisis Response and Management*, 7(4), 1–25. doi:10.4018/IJISCRAM.2015100101

Hernandez, M. W. (2014). A Multiple Natural Hazards Assessment Model Based on Geomorphic Terrain Units. *International Journal of Applied Geospatial Research*, 5(1), 16–37. doi:10.4018/ijagr.2014010102

Hewitt, A. M., Wagner, S. L., Twal, R., & Gourley, D. (2015). Aligning Community Hospitals with Local Public Health Departments: Collaborative Emergency Management. In M. Hamner, S. Stovall, D. Taha, & S. Brahimi (Eds.), *Emergency Management and Disaster Response Utilizing Public-Private Partnerships* (pp. 218–239). Hershey, PA: IGI Global. doi:10.4018/978-1-4666-8159-0.ch012

Howard-Baptiste, S., & Baptiste, M. (2015). Piti, Piti, Wazo fe Nich Li (Little by Little, the Bird Builds its Nest): Promoting Change and Health Education in Post-Earthquake Haiti. In J. Bird (Ed.), *Innovative Collaborative Practice and Reflection in Patient Education* (pp. 129–151). Hershey, PA: IGI Global. doi:10.4018/978-1-4666-7524-7.ch009

Jones, A. (2016). Shortcomings and Successes: A Small-Scale Disaster Case Study. In E. Decker & J. Townes (Eds.), *Handbook of Research on Disaster Management and Contingency Planning in Modern Libraries* (pp. 412–435). Hershey, PA: IGI Global. doi:10.4018/978-1-4666-8624-3.ch018

Joshi, S., Gupta, I. D., Pattanur, L. R., & Murnal, P. B. (2014). Investigating the Effect of Depth and Impedance of Foundation Rock in Seismic Analysis of Gravity Dams. *International Journal of Geotechnical Earthquake Engineering*, 5(2), 1–18. doi:10.4018/ijgee.2014070101

Karl, I., Rother, K., & Nestler, S. (2015). Crisis-Related Apps: Assistance for Critical and Emergency Situations. *International Journal of Information Systems for Crisis Response and Management*, 7(2), 19–35. doi:10.4018/IJISCRAM.2015040102

Kumar, A., Mukherjee, A. B., & Krishna, A. P. (2017). Application of Conventional Data Mining Techniques and Web Mining to Aid Disaster Management. In A. Kumar (Ed.), *Web Usage Mining Techniques and Applications Across Industries* (pp. 138–167). Hershey, PA: IGI Global. doi:10.4018/978-1-5225-0613-3.ch006

Kumar, C. P. (2016). Impact of Climate Change on Groundwater Resources. In S. Dinda (Ed.), *Handbook of Research on Climate Change Impact on Health and Environmental Sustainability* (pp. 196–221). Hershey, PA: IGI Global. doi:10.4018/978-1-4666-8814-8.ch010

Kurata, N., Ohashi, M., & Hori, M. (2015). Local Communities Platform for Restoration of "Kizuna": Reconstruction of Human Bonds in Communities Damaged by Nuclear Disaster. In J. Varajão, M. Cruz-Cunha, & R. Martinho (Eds.), *Improving Organizational Effectiveness with Enterprise Information Systems* (pp. 123–136). Hershey, PA: IGI Global. doi:10.4018/978-1-4666-8368-6.ch008

Kurki, T., & Sihvonen, H. (2014). Operative Role Management in Information Systems. In Z. Mahmood (Ed.), *IT in the Public Sphere: Applications in Administration, Government, Politics, and Planning* (pp. 1–17). Hershey, PA: IGI Global. doi:10.4018/978-1-4666-4719-0.ch001

Kurki, T., & Sihvonen, H. (2014). Operative Role Management in Information Systems. In Z. Mahmood (Ed.), *IT in the Public Sphere: Applications in Administration, Government, Politics, and Planning* (pp. 1–17). Hershey, PA: IGI Global. doi:10.4018/978-1-4666-4719-0.ch001

Kushwaha, D., Janagam, S., & Trivedi, N. (2014). Compute-Efficient Geo-Localization of Targets from UAV Videos: Real-Time Processing in Unknown Territory. *International Journal of Applied Geospatial Research*, 5(3), 36–48. doi:10.4018/ijagr.2014070103

Lee, C., & Wu, C. (2015). Extracting Entities of Emergent Events from Social Streams Based on a Data-Cluster Slicing Approach for Ontology Engineering. *International Journal of Information Retrieval Research*, 5(3), 1–18. doi:10.4018/IJIRR.2015070101

Leh, J. M. (2016). The RSVP Model: Lifting the Veil on School Violence. In G. Crews (Ed.), *Critical Examinations of School Violence and Disturbance in K-12 Education* (pp. 234–256). Hershey, PA: IGI Global. doi:10.4018/978-1-4666-9935-9.ch014

Leung, L., & Law, N. (2016). Exploring the Effectiveness of Online Role Play Simulations in Tackling Groupthink in Crisis Management Training. *International Journal of Gaming and Computer-Mediated Simulations*, 8(3), 1–18. doi:10.4018/IJGCMS.2016070101 PMID:27134698

Lindahl, J., Bett, B., Robinson, T., & Grace, D. (2017). Rift Valley Fever and the Changing Environment: A Case Study in East Africa. In M. Bouzid (Ed.), *Examining the Role of Environmental Change on Emerging Infectious Diseases and Pandemics* (pp. 178–204). Hershey, PA: IGI Global. doi:10.4018/978-1-5225-0553-2.ch008

Lock, M. B., Fansler, C., & Webb, M. (2016). Emergency Planning (R)Evolution: Making a Comprehensive Emergency Plan for the Present and the Future. In E. Decker & J. Townes (Eds.), *Handbook of Research on Disaster Management and Contingency Planning in Modern Libraries* (pp. 70–95). Hershey, PA: IGI Global. doi:10.4018/978-1-4666-8624-3.ch004

Lorenzi, D., Chun, S. A., Vaidya, J., Shafiq, B., Atluri, V., & Adam, N. R. (2015). PEER: A Framework for Public Engagement in Emergency Response. *International Journal of E-Planning Research*, 4(3), 29–46. doi:10.4018/IJEPR.2015070102

Lowe, M., Matthews, M., Reno, L. M., & Sartori, M. A. (2016). The LOUIS Consortium and Catastrophe. In B. Doherty (Ed.), *Technology-Centered Academic Library Partnerships and Collaborations* (pp. 126–166). Hershey, PA: IGI Global. doi:10.4018/978-1-5225-0323-1.ch005

Mabe, M. R. (2016). Libraries to the Rescue. *International Journal of Risk and Contingency Management*, 5(1), 62–81. doi:10.4018/IJRCM.2016010105

Mabe, M. R. (2016). The Library as Lifeboat. In E. Decker & J. Townes (Eds.), *Handbook of Research on Disaster Management and Contingency Planning in Modern Libraries* (pp. 494–515). Hershey, PA: IGI Global. doi:10.4018/978-1-4666-8624-3.ch021

Related Readings

Machalaba, C., Romanelli, C., & Stoett, P. (2017). Global Environmental Change and Emerging Infectious Diseases: Macrolevel Drivers and Policy Responses. In M. Bouzid (Ed.), *Examining the Role of Environmental Change on Emerging Infectious Diseases and Pandemics* (pp. 24–67). Hershey, PA: IGI Global. doi:10.4018/978-1-5225-0553-2.ch002

Maftei, C., & Papatheodorou, K. (2015). Mathematical Models Used for Hydrological Floodplain Modeling. In C. Maftei (Ed.), *Extreme Weather and Impacts of Climate Change on Water Resources in the Dobrogea Region* (pp. 240–283). Hershey, PA: IGI Global. doi:10.4018/978-1-4666-8438-6.ch009

Magda, B. (2015). Communications and Information Sharing in Public-Private Partnerships: Networking for Emergency Management. In M. Hamner, S. Stovall, D. Taha, & S. Brahimi (Eds.), *Emergency Management and Disaster Response Utilizing Public-Private Partnerships* (pp. 162–182). Hershey, PA: IGI Global. doi:10.4018/978-1-4666-8159-0.ch009

Maharaj, R., Singh-Ackbarali, D., & Sankat, C. K. (2015). Postharvest Management Strategies. In W. Ganpat & W. Isaac (Eds.), *Impacts of Climate Change on Food Security in Small Island Developing States* (pp. 221–254). Hershey, PA: IGI Global. doi:10.4018/978-1-4666-6501-9.ch008

Mahdi, T. (2015). Seismic Vulnerability of Arches, Vaults and Domes in Historical Buildings. In P. Asteris & V. Plevris (Eds.), *Handbook of Research on Seismic Assessment and Rehabilitation of Historic Structures* (pp. 401–447). Hershey, PA: IGI Global. doi:10.4018/978-1-4666-8286-3.ch014

Matsumura, N., Miura, A., Komori, M., & Hiraishi, K. (2016). Media Mediate Sentiments: Exploratory Analysis of Tweets Posted Before, During, and After the Great East Japan Earthquake. *International Journal of Knowledge Society Research*, 7(2), 57–71. doi:10.4018/IJKSR.2016040104

Maximay, S. (2015). The Caribbean's Response to Climate Change Impacts. In W. Ganpat & W. Isaac (Eds.), *Impacts of Climate Change on Food Security in Small Island Developing States* (pp. 33–66). Hershey, PA: IGI Global. doi:10.4018/978-1-4666-6501-9.ch002

Meesters, K., & Van de Walle, B. (2014). Serious Gaming for User Centered Innovation and Adoption of Disaster Response Information Systems. *International Journal of Information Systems for Crisis Response and Management*, 6(2), 1–15. doi:10.4018/ijiscram.2014040101

Mohan Babu, K. N., Murthy, K. B., Pavithra, G., & Mamatha, K. (2014). Efficient Channel Utilization and Prioritization Scheme for Emergency Calls in Cellular Network. *International Journal of Wireless Networks and Broadband Technologies*, *3*(3), 56–69. doi:10.4018/ijwnbt.2014070104

Mondlane, A., Hasson, K., & Popov, O. (2015). E-Governance and Natural Hazards in Mozambique: A Challenge for Backasting Method Used for Flood Risk Management Strategies. In I. Sodhi (Ed.), *Emerging Issues and Prospects in African E-Government* (pp. 253–268). Hershey, PA: IGI Global. doi:10.4018/978-1-4666-6296-4.ch016

Moon, T., & Ko, S. (2015). Compassion Organizing for Public-Private Collaboration in Disaster Management. In M. Hamner, S. Stovall, D. Taha, & S. Brahimi (Eds.), *Emergency Management and Disaster Response Utilizing Public-Private Partnerships* (pp. 99–120). Hershey, PA: IGI Global. doi:10.4018/978-1-4666-8159-0.ch006

Mukherjee, A., Dey, N., Kausar, N., Ashour, A. S., Taiar, R., & Hassanien, A. E. (2016). A Disaster Management Specific Mobility Model for Flying Ad-hoc Network. *International Journal of Rough Sets and Data Analysis*, *3*(3), 72–103. doi:10.4018/IJRSDA.2016070106

Murayama, Y., Nishioka, D., & Abdullah, N. A. (2016). Information Processing for Disaster Communications. In A. Aggarwal (Ed.), *Managing Big Data Integration in the Public Sector* (pp. 207–230). Hershey, PA: IGI Global. doi:10.4018/978-1-4666-9649-5.ch012

Negron, M. (2015). Use Team Building to Make the Most of Your Public-Private Partnerships. In M. Hamner, S. Stovall, D. Taha, & S. Brahimi (Eds.), *Emergency Management and Disaster Response Utilizing Public-Private Partnerships* (pp. 121–135). Hershey, PA: IGI Global. doi:10.4018/978-1-4666-8159-0.ch007

Negrón, M. A., & Taha, D. (2015). Public-Private Partnerships in Support of Critical Infrastructure and Key Resources. In M. Hamner, S. Stovall, D. Taha, & S. Brahimi (Eds.), *Emergency Management and Disaster Response Utilizing Public-Private Partnerships* (pp. 256–269). Hershey, PA: IGI Global. doi:10.4018/978-1-4666-8159-0.ch014

Ngamassi, L., Ramakrishnan, T., & Rahman, S. (2016). Use of Social Media for Disaster Management: A Prescriptive Framework. *Journal of Organizational and End User Computing*, *28*(3), 122–140. doi:10.4018/JOEUC.2016070108

Nikolai, C., Johnson, T., Prietula, M., Becerra-Fernandez, I., & Madey, G. (2015). SimEOC: A Distributed Web-Based Virtual Emergency Operations Center Simulator for Training and Research. *International Journal of Information Systems for Crisis Response and Management*, *7*(1), 1–21. doi:10.4018/IJISCRAM.2015010101

Related Readings

Nikolai, C. M., Johnson, T., Prietula, M., Becerra-Fernandez, I., & Madey, G. R. (2015). Design Principles for Crisis Information Management Systems: From Closed Local Systems to the Web and Beyond. *International Journal of Information Systems for Crisis Response and Management, 7*(4), 26–45. doi:10.4018/IJISCRAM.2015100102

Nixon, M. L. (2016). Safety Doesn't Happen by Accident: Disaster Planning at the University of Pittsburgh. In E. Decker & J. Townes (Eds.), *Handbook of Research on Disaster Management and Contingency Planning in Modern Libraries* (pp. 184–206). Hershey, PA: IGI Global. doi:10.4018/978-1-4666-8624-3.ch009

Noble, K. T., White, C., & Turoff, M. (2014). Emergency Management Information System Support Rectifying First Responder Role Abandonment During Extreme Events. *International Journal of Information Systems for Crisis Response and Management, 6*(1), 65–78. doi:10.4018/ijiscram.2014010103

Noblin, A. M., Cortelyou-Ward, K., & Rutherford, A. (2016). Weathering the Storm: Disaster Preparedness and the Florida Health Information Exchange. *International Journal of Privacy and Health Information Management, 4*(2), 53–61. doi:10.4018/IJPHIM.2016070104

Okada, A., Ishida, Y., & Yamauchi, N. (2017). Effectiveness of Social Media in Disaster Fundraising: Mobilizing the Public towards Voluntary Actions. *International Journal of Public Administration in the Digital Age, 4*(1), 49–68. doi:10.4018/IJPADA.2017010104

Panwar, N., Uniyal, D., & Rautela, K. S. (2016). Mapping Sustainable Tourism into Emergency Management Structure to Enhance Humanitarian Networks and Disaster Risk Reduction using Public-Private Partnerships (PPP) Initiatives in Himalayan States: The Global Supply Chain Issues and Strategies. In S. Joshi & R. Joshi (Eds.), *Designing and Implementing Global Supply Chain Management* (pp. 129–151). Hershey, PA: IGI Global. doi:10.4018/978-1-4666-9720-1.ch007

Patkin, T. T. (2017). Social Media and Knowledge Management in a Crisis Context: Barriers and Opportunities. In R. Chugh (Ed.), *Harnessing Social Media as a Knowledge Management Tool* (pp. 125–142). Hershey, PA: IGI Global. doi:10.4018/978-1-5225-0495-5.ch007

Piper, J., & Müller, B. (2016). Modular Technical Concepts for Ambulatory Monitoring of Risk Patients Based on Multiple Parameters and an Automatic Alarm Function. *International Journal of Monitoring and Surveillance Technologies Research, 4*(1), 1–9. doi:10.4018/IJMSTR.2016010101

Purohit, H., Dalal, M., Singh, P., Nissima, B., Moorthy, V., Vemuri, A., & Rajgaria, A. et al. (2016). Empowering Crisis Response-Led Citizen Communities: Lessons Learned from JKFloodRelief.org Initiative. In C. Graham (Ed.), *Strategic Management and Leadership for Systems Development in Virtual Spaces* (pp. 270–292). Hershey, PA: IGI Global. doi:10.4018/978-1-4666-9688-4.ch015

Radianti, J., Granmo, O., Bouhmala, N., Sarshar, P., & Gonzalez, J. J. (2014). Comparing Different Crowd Emergency Evacuation Models Based on Human Centered Sensing Criteria. *International Journal of Information Systems for Crisis Response and Management, 6*(3), 53–70. doi:10.4018/IJISCRAM.2014070104

Rastrick, K., Stahl, F., Vossen, G., & Dillon, S. (2015). WiPo for SAR: Taking the Web in Your Pocket when Doing Search and Rescue in New Zealand. *International Journal of Information Systems for Crisis Response and Management, 7*(4), 46–66. doi:10.4018/IJISCRAM.2015100103

Reginaldi, J. (2015). Leadership Challenges in Public Private Partnerships in Emergency Management: A Real-World Perspective. In M. Hamner, S. Stovall, D. Taha, & S. Brahimi (Eds.), *Emergency Management and Disaster Response Utilizing Public-Private Partnerships* (pp. 136–161). Hershey, PA: IGI Global. doi:10.4018/978-1-4666-8159-0.ch008

Reuter, C. (2014). Communication between Power Blackout and Mobile Network Overload. *International Journal of Information Systems for Crisis Response and Management, 6*(2), 38–53. doi:10.4018/ijiscram.2014040103

Reuter, C., Ludwig, T., Friberg, T., Pratzler-Wanczura, S., & Gizikis, A. (2015). Social Media and Emergency Services?: Interview Study on Current and Potential Use in 7 European Countries. *International Journal of Information Systems for Crisis Response and Management, 7*(2), 36–58. doi:10.4018/IJISCRAM.2015040103

Reuter, C., & Schröter, J. (2015). Microblogging during the European Floods 2013: What Twitter May Contribute in German Emergencies. *International Journal of Information Systems for Crisis Response and Management, 7*(1), 22–41. doi:10.4018/IJISCRAM.2015010102

Rich, E., Hernantes, J., Laugé, A., Labaka, L., Sarriegi, J. M., & Gonzalez, J. J. (2014). Improving the Crisis to Crisis Learning Process. *International Journal of Information Systems for Crisis Response and Management, 6*(3), 38–52. doi:10.4018/ijiscram.2014070103

Related Readings

Rizza, C., Pereira, Â. G., & Curvelo, P. (2014). Do-it-Yourself Justice: Considerations of Social Media use in a Crisis Situation: The Case of the 2011 Vancouver Riots. *International Journal of Information Systems for Crisis Response and Management*, *6*(4), 42–59. doi:10.4018/IJISCRAM.2014100104

Roberts, T. G., & Rodriguez, M. T. (2015). An Overview of Climate Change and Impacts on Food Security in Small Island Developing States. In W. Ganpat & W. Isaac (Eds.), *Impacts of Climate Change on Food Security in Small Island Developing States* (pp. 1–31). Hershey, PA: IGI Global. doi:10.4018/978-1-4666-6501-9.ch001

Roşu, L., & Zăgan, R. (2015). Management of Drought and Floods in Romania. In C. Maftei (Ed.), *Extreme Weather and Impacts of Climate Change on Water Resources in the Dobrogea Region* (pp. 345–402). Hershey, PA: IGI Global. doi:10.4018/978-1-4666-8438-6.ch012

Rother, K., Karl, I., & Nestler, S. (2015). Towards Virtual Reality Crisis Simulation as a Tool for Usability Testing of Crisis Related Interactive Systems. *International Journal of Information Systems for Crisis Response and Management*, *7*(3), 40–54. doi:10.4018/IJISCRAM.2015070103

Russo, M. R., Bryan, V., & Penney, G. (2014). The Learning Curve in Emergency Preparedness: Are We Getting Better? In M. Khosrow-Pour (Ed.), *Inventive Approaches for Technology Integration and Information Resources Management* (pp. 278–293). Hershey, PA: IGI Global. doi:10.4018/978-1-4666-6256-8.ch012

Sarhosis, V., Lignola, G. P., & Asteris, P. G. (2015). Seismic Vulnerability of Ancient Colonnade: Two Story Colonnade of the Forum in Pompeii. In P. Asteris & V. Plevris (Eds.), *Handbook of Research on Seismic Assessment and Rehabilitation of Historic Structures* (pp. 331–358). Hershey, PA: IGI Global. doi:10.4018/978-1-4666-8286-3.ch011

Sautter, J., Havlik, D., Böspflug, L., Max, M., Rannat, K., Erlich, M., & Engelbach, W. (2015). Simulation and Analysis of Mass Casualty Mission Tactics: Context of Use, Interaction Concept, Agent-Based Model and Evaluation. *International Journal of Information Systems for Crisis Response and Management*, *7*(3), 16–39. doi:10.4018/IJISCRAM.2015070102

Scholl, H. J., & Chatfield, A. T. (2014). The Role of Resilient Information Infrastructures: The Case of Radio Fukushima During and After the 2011 Eastern Japan Catastrophe. *International Journal of Public Administration in the Digital Age*, *1*(2), 1–24. doi:10.4018/ijpada.2014040101

Schryen, G., & Wex, F. (2014). Risk Reduction in Natural Disaster Management Through Information Systems: A Literature Review and an IS Design Science Research Agenda. *International Journal of Information Systems for Crisis Response and Management, 6*(1), 38–64. doi:10.4018/ijiscram.2014010102

Senapati, S., & Gupta, V. (2016). Impacts of Climate Change on Fish Productivity: A Quantitative Measurement. In S. Dinda (Ed.), *Handbook of Research on Climate Change Impact on Health and Environmental Sustainability* (pp. 243–260). Hershey, PA: IGI Global. doi:10.4018/978-1-4666-8814-8.ch012

Shaw, M. D. (2016). Navigating Campus Disasters from Within the Library: Lessons and Implications from Gulf Coast Institutions. In E. Decker & J. Townes (Eds.), *Handbook of Research on Disaster Management and Contingency Planning in Modern Libraries* (pp. 340–365). Hershey, PA: IGI Global. doi:10.4018/978-1-4666-8624-3.ch015

Shiuly, A., Sahu, R. B., & Mandal, S. (2014). Effect of Soil on Ground Motion Amplification of Kolkata City. *International Journal of Geotechnical Earthquake Engineering, 5*(1), 1–20. doi:10.4018/ijgee.2014010101

Sönmez, R. (2017). Value Creation through Social Alliances: Theoretical Considerations in Partnership Relationships. In V. Potocan, M. Üngan, & Z. Nedelko (Eds.), *Handbook of Research on Managerial Solutions in Non-Profit Organizations* (pp. 205–231). Hershey, PA: IGI Global. doi:10.4018/978-1-5225-0731-4.ch010

Steinbuch, R. (2015). Optimization of Tuned Mass Dampers to Improve the Earthquake Resistance of High Buildings. In N. Gaurina-Medjimurec (Ed.), *Handbook of Research on Advancements in Environmental Engineering* (pp. 511–548). Hershey, PA: IGI Global. doi:10.4018/978-1-4666-7336-6.ch018

Swain, M. (2016). Vulnerability to Local Climate Change: Farmers' Perceptions on Trends in Western Odisha, India. In S. Dinda (Ed.), *Handbook of Research on Climate Change Impact on Health and Environmental Sustainability* (pp. 139–155). Hershey, PA: IGI Global. doi:10.4018/978-1-4666-8814-8.ch007

Taha, D. (2015). Mitigating the Impact of Extreme Events: A Private Sector Perspective on the Value of Public Private Partnerships. In M. Hamner, S. Stovall, D. Taha, & S. Brahimi (Eds.), *Emergency Management and Disaster Response Utilizing Public-Private Partnerships* (pp. 32–53). Hershey, PA: IGI Global. doi:10.4018/978-1-4666-8159-0.ch003

Related Readings

Takayama, Y., & Miwa, H. (2015). Delay Tolerant Navigation Method for Fast Evacuation in Poor Communication Environment at the Time of Disaster. *International Journal of Distributed Systems and Technologies*, 6(3), 29–50. doi:10.4018/IJDST.2015070103

Tapia, A. H., Giacobe, N. A., Soule, P. J., & LaLone, N. J. (2016). Scaling 911 Texting for Large-Scale Disasters: Developing Practical Technical Innovations for Emergency Management at Public Universities. *International Journal of Public Administration in the Digital Age*, 3(3), 73–85. doi:10.4018/IJPADA.2016070105

Treurniet, W. (2014). Shaping Comprehensive Emergency Response Networks. In T. Grant, R. Janssen, & H. Monsuur (Eds.), *Network Topology in Command and Control: Organization, Operation, and Evolution* (pp. 26–48). Hershey, PA: IGI Global. doi:10.4018/978-1-4666-6058-8.ch002

Trnka, J., & Johansson, B. J. (2014). Resilient Emergency Response: Supporting Flexibility and Improvisation in Collaborative Command and Control. In *Crisis Management: Concepts, Methodologies, Tools, and Applications* (pp. 813–838). Hershey, PA: IGI Global. doi:10.4018/978-1-4666-4707-7.ch040

Vandevoordt, R. (2016). Humanitarian Media Events: On the Symbolic Conditions of Moral Integration. In A. Fox (Ed.), *Global Perspectives on Media Events in Contemporary Society* (pp. 90–105). Hershey, PA: IGI Global. doi:10.4018/978-1-4666-9967-0.ch007

Venkatesan, S., Rajabifard, A., Lam, N., Gad, E., Goldsworthy, H., & Griffin, G. (2014). A Syncretic Approach Towards a Meta-Integrative Platform for Effective Disaster Management. *International Journal of Geotechnical Earthquake Engineering*, 5(1), 58–74. doi:10.4018/ijgee.2014010104

Verplaetse, A., Mascareñas, P., & O'Neill, K. (2016). Zen and the Art of Disaster Planning: Collaboration Challenges in Library Disaster Plan Design and Execution. In E. Decker & J. Townes (Eds.), *Handbook of Research on Disaster Management and Contingency Planning in Modern Libraries* (pp. 96–119). Hershey, PA: IGI Global. doi:10.4018/978-1-4666-8624-3.ch005

Vezyridis, P., Timmons, S., & Wharrad, H. (2016). Lessons Learned from the Implementation of an Emergency Department Information System. In T. Iyamu & A. Tatnall (Eds.), *Maximizing Healthcare Delivery and Management through Technology Integration* (pp. 237–256). Hershey, PA: IGI Global. doi:10.4018/978-1-4666-9446-0.ch014

Vorraber, W., Lichtenegger, G., Brugger, J., Gojmerac, I., Egly, M., Panzenböck, K., & Voessner, S. et al. (2016). Designing Information Systems to Facilitate Civil-Military Cooperation in Disaster Management. *International Journal of Distributed Systems and Technologies*, 7(4), 22–40. doi:10.4018/IJDST.2016100102

Wridt, P., Seley, J. E., Fisher, S., & DuBois, B. (2014). Participatory Mapping Approaches to Coordinate the Emergency Response of Spontaneous Volunteers After Hurricane Sandy. *International Journal of E-Planning Research*, 3(3), 1–19. doi:10.4018/ijepr.2014070101

Yildiz, M., & Demirhan, K. (2016). Analysis and Comparison of the Role of Local Governments with Other Policy Actors in Disaster Relief via Social Media: The Case of Turkey. In U. Sadioglu & K. Dede (Eds.), *Theoretical Foundations and Discussions on the Reformation Process in Local Governments* (pp. 462–483). Hershey, PA: IGI Global. doi:10.4018/978-1-5225-0317-0.ch019

Young-McLear, K., Mazzuchi, T. A., & Sarkani, S. (2015). Large-Scale Disaster Response Management: Social Media and Homeland Security. In J. Sahlin (Ed.), *Social Media and the Transformation of Interaction in Society* (pp. 93–131). Hershey, PA: IGI Global. doi:10.4018/978-1-4666-8556-7.ch006

About the Author

John McCaskill completed his PhD in 2012 from the University of Texas at Dallas where he serves as a Clinical Professor in the department of Public and Nonprofit Management. He is an honor graduate of the United States Army War College. John's current research interests and publications focus on sustainability and the resilience of public and nonprofit organizations under stress. John's previous publications examine U.S. national security with regard to energy policy. His professional background includes over 20 years of military service as well as 17 years in the building products industry specializing in sustainable building products. John's design work in the building products industry has resulted in the award of five patents.

Index

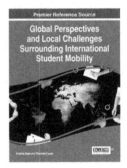

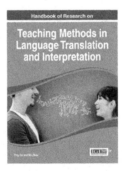
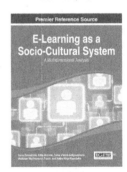

Stay Current on the Latest Emerging Research Developments

Become an IGI Global Reviewer for Authored Book Projects

Premier Reference Source

Solutions for High-Touch Communications in a High-Tech World

Premier Reference Source

Advanced Research on Biologically Inspired Cognitive Architectures

Premier Reference Source

Workforce Development Theory and Practice in the Mental Health Sector

Premier Reference Source

Resource Management and Efficiency in Cloud Computing Environments

The overall success of an authored book project is dependent on quality and timely reviews.

In this competitive age of scholarly publishing, constructive and timely feedback significantly decreases the turnaround time of manuscripts from submission to acceptance, allowing the publication and discovery of progressive research at a much more expeditious rate. Several IGI Global authored book projects are currently seeking highly qualified experts in the field to fill vacancies on their respective editorial review boards:

Applications may be sent to:
development@igi-global.com

Applicants must have a doctorate (or an equivalent degree) as well as publishing and reviewing experience. Reviewers are asked to write reviews in a timely, collegial, and constructive manner. All reviewers will begin their role on an ad-hoc basis for a period of one year, and upon successful completion of this term can be considered for full editorial review board status, with the potential for a subsequent promotion to Associate Editor.

If you have a colleague that may be interested in this opportunity, we encourage you to share this information with them.

Encyclopedia of Information Science and Technology, Third Edition (10 Vols.)

Mehdi Khosrow-Pour, D.B.A. (Information Resources Management Association, USA)
ISBN: 978-1-4666-5888-2; **EISBN:** 978-1-4666-5889-9; © 2015; 10,384 pages.

The **Encyclopedia of Information Science and Technology, Third Edition** is a 10-volume compilation of authoritative, previously unpublished research-based articles contributed by thousands of researchers and experts from all over the world. This discipline-defining encyclopedia will serve research needs in numerous fields that are affected by the rapid pace and substantial impact of technological change. With an emphasis on modern issues and the presentation of potential opportunities, prospective solutions, and future directions in the field, it is a relevant and essential addition to any academic library's reference collection.

Take An Extra

30% Off[1]

Free Lifetime E-Access with Print Purchase

Take 30% Off Retail Price:

Hardcover with Free E-Access:[2] **$2,765**
List Price: $3,950

E-Access with Free Hardcover:[2] **$2,765**
List Price: $3,950

E-Subscription Price:

One (1) Year E-Subscription: $1,288
List Price: $1,840

Two (2) Year E-Subscription: $2,177
List Price: $3,110

Recommend this Title to Your Institution's Library: www.igi-global.com/books

Printed in the United States
By Bookmasters